PERTENÆCER:

Eight-Week Mindfulness and Meditation Training and Practices for Latinx Immigrants in the United States.

By: *Criss A. Cuervo*

Illustrations by: Amanda Ng Yann Chwen
Format and Edits by: María José Jaramillo

Dedication

Este proyecto está dedicado a mis padres, Hugo y Martha, quienes me han apoyado en este camino a pertenecer a mí misma y quienes me enseñaron el concepto de ser ciudadana del mundo. Los quiero, gracias por su amor y apoyo, me ha demostrado lo que es el amor incondicional.

[This project is dedicated to my parents, Hugo and Martha, who have supported me in my journey to belong to myself and who taught me the concept of being a citizen of the world. I love you, thank you for your love and support, you have shown me what unconditional love is.]

A mi pareja de vida, Juan Sebastián, quien me ha apoyado en todos los sentidos y quien me ha enseñado a ser paciente, perseverar y luchar por mi vocación en la vida.

[To my life partner, Juan Sebastián, who has supported me in all senses and who has taught me to be patient, persevere and fight for my vocation in life.]

También se la dedico a todos los inmigrantes del mundo, que, como yo y mis padres, han dejado su tierra para buscar un futuro mejor para ellos y para sus familias.

[I also dedicate it to all the immigrants of the world, who, like me and my parents, have left their land to look for a better future for themselves and their families.]

Table of Contents

About the Author

A Latinx wanting to enhance the way we think, feel and live!
I was born and raised in Venezuela. My parents immigrated from
Colombia in their mid-twenties. In 1998, my parents encountered the
opportunity to migrate to the United States legally. Since then I have
lived throughout the United States, in places like Houston, Texas;
Springfield, Illinois; Miami, Florida; and Bristol, Connecticut; I have also
had the chance to travel extensively and live in places like Queretaro,
Mexico, and currently Toledo, Spain.

Since I was a little girl I wanted to be a news anchor; however, in
1998 my plans came to a halt when my parents decided to immigrate to a
new country with a different language and culture. Slowly, I was able to
work my way through a new culture, language, and location. In 2004, I
graduated with a Bachelor of Arts with an emphasis in Communications
from the University of Illinois at Springfield (UIS), and from 2005 until
2008, I found a way to pursue my dreams, so I moved to Miami, Florida

and completed graduate courses in Spanish Language journalism at the University of Miami and Florida International University.

Professionally, I worked in various departments of the television industry where I received multiple awards for my leadership, performance, and innovative skills. However, my dreams to be a news anchor were becoming buried by my fears, insecurities, and anxieties. A few years into my career in the industry, a series of events led me towards taking a shift in my life and career. I will expand on these throughout the guide.

In 2015, I founded AlmayEspiritu.com, a socially responsible business with the mission to promote mindfulness and meditation practices in Latinx communities and workplaces. In May 2019, I will be completing a Master of Arts in Mindfulness from Lesley University in Cambridge, Massachusetts. This curriculum is presented as a representation of my inner work and transformation throughout this program and in my life.

Through the practice of meditation, mindfulness, and cultivation of knowledge I have been able to change the way I feel, think, and act in the world. For many years, my motto was 'work hard, play hard.' This way of thinking and living led me to some professional success; however, it also led me to forget and care for my mental and emotional health. The emptiness and stress I felt in my life manifested itself through anxiety and anxiety attacks; reading, meditating, and applying mindfulness in my life have given me the ability to cultivate self-love, compassion, and wisdom. These are essential tools for meaningful, long-lasting success and happiness.

In my free time, you can find me meditating, reading, philosophizing, or just being with nature. I also love D-I-Y art projects, walking without a purpose, and play a good tennis match!

Mental Health Note: Please know that I am not a certified mental health professional; if you are experiencing unmanageable emotions, thoughts, and/or sensations, please visit Appendix C and reach out to local mental health professional. I encourage to do so, I have personally attended therapy, and it was the best decision I could have ever made.

About this Guidebook

In this eight-week curriculum guide book, readers and participants learn about the importance of mental health hygiene through the study of mental health, the mind, common mental health stigmas in the Latinx community, and the use of culturally-attuned meditation and mindfulness practices as mental health hygiene tools. The curriculum helps the reader to work through his/her/their acculturative stress triggers and manifestations. Some of the culturally-adapted mindfulness practices revolve around connecting with their ancestry, writing about their migration circumstances, and finding cultural affinities. Some of the meditative practices help readers learn to identify negative patterns and habits, learn about emotions, learn how to apply self-regulation and breathing techniques, and cultivate self-love, empathy, and self-compassion to heal and prevent long term effects on their mental health. The overall goal of this curriculum is to allow readers and practitioners to manage their stress and leave with a sense of belonging to themselves, their families, their communities, and their country - the United States.

Curriculum Objectives

- Importance of mental health hygiene
- Understanding the mind and the subjective experience
- Common mental health stigmas and idioms used in the Latinx community
- Understanding of acculturative stress and ties to discrimination, language proficiency, and migration circumstances
- Open to new perspectives on life and life circumstances
- Learn culturally-attuned Meditation and mindfulness practices
- Learn about self-regulation

- Understanding of basic emotions: Fear, Anger, Sadness, and Joy
- Cultivation of compassion and empathy
- Ability to identify unhealthy habits and patterns of the mind/subjective experience
- Understanding Interconnectedness
- Understanding Shame
- Build a strong sense of belonging in their communities, the United States or anywhere they may be

Why Pertenæcer?

The title of this curriculum and training was chosen based on the need and yearning of all immigrants and humans to belong. The word *pertenæcer* means to belong in English; I have purposefully chosen the Latin alphabet letter æ[1], because it acknowledges the Latin roots of the Spanish language, and most importantly it allows us in this training to create two words out of one. The first being *Pertenæcer* - to belong and the second *nacer* – to be born. The reason for this was to give the reader and participant the opportunity to be reborn and to give birth to new ways of being and living so they can cope with acculturative stressors and therefore feel like they belong to themselves, their families, their communities, and their country, the United States.

Is this for Me?

This guidebook is designed for everyone. Nevertheless, it may resonate better with bilingual millennials (born between the early 1980s to early 2000s) and college-educated Latinx late-immigrants (someone who immigrated over the age of 15) in the United States. This mental health hygiene tools guidebook is best for those that are not experiencing unbearable mental or physical distress.

As the author, I chose to use the term Latinx[1,2] throughout this guide as a way to show my openness and welcoming language to all the readers. As most people know, the Latinx community in the United States is very diverse. Therefore, this term will be used as a label for a group that is hard to define. The intent in this course was to choose a word that represents and integrates such a distinct group without limitations and welcomes its diversity, its cultures, its nationalities, its ethnicities, its sexual-orientations, its gender identifications, its races, and any other forms of self-identification.

This guidebook has been designed with the US Latinx immigrant diversity of nationalities, races, and cultures in mind. It is important also to note that we have taken into consideration that some immigrants may share some factors, each individual has a unique and special story. To help you identify better with this program, please take some time to answer fill-out the following questionnaire. **If you answer YES to at least 5 of them, this guidebook is for you!**

Check YES if it applies to you, and NO if it doesn't	YES	NO
1. My well-being and happiness are important, as well as the well-being and happiness of my family	✓	
2. Support from my family is important during stressful times; however, there are times that I wish I had more tools and support		✓
3. Leaving my home-country left me without emotional support	✓	
4. Life in the united states has been extremely different than expected	✓	

5. People treat me different because I am an immigrant	✓	
6. I need tools to cope with discrimination and being an immigrant in the United States	✓	
7. I want to learn new practices that value my culture and my traditions	✓	
8. I migrated to the united states at the age of 15 or older	✓	
9. Leaving my country has been very difficult	✓	
10. I feel like I don't belong or fit-in in the United States	✓	
11. At times I feel lonely and isolated in the United States		✓
12. I am ashamed of my accent	✓	
13. I am ashamed of my culture and my ancestry		✓
14. I don't understand the American culture, but I would like to understand more	✓	
15. It is hard for me to make friends in the United States		✓

Source: See notes[3]

How to Use this Guidebook

This guidebook is to be used as a personal step-by-step instruction book in eight consecutive weeks. The ideal setting is to complete simultaneously with an online-live or in-person group learning environment. (You can sign up for a session on www.almayespiritu.com.) The learning approach is inspired by Paulo Freire's pedagogical approach of self-inquiry and reflection, as well as author narratives to help the reader connect and identify acculturative stress and feelings of not belonging. The guidebook should be used as a self-guided, and the user has the opportunity to revisit the exercises and content at any time. Anyone wanting to teach a generic version of this curriculum should contact the author to get certification and permission to impart the curriculum.

Each week has a topic and theme. After each class, the student has seven (7) days until the next chapter to:

- Complete readings
- Complete reflections from each section
  - Use *Mindful Journaling* practices for your written reflections - This type of writing invites intellectual discursive considerations and reflections on thought patterns, sensations, and emotions[1].
- Take a break to reflect on the *Dichos* (proverbs/sayings) and quotes throughout the guidebook (You may do solo mental reflections, however, reflecting with others in conversation is encouraged)
- Practice assigned mindfulness activities
- Practice guided meditations

  o Audio available online:
     www.almayespiritu.com/guidedmeditations
     ▪ Password to access: pertenæcer
- If the student has joined an in-person or online group, he/she/they should complete assigned sharing practices.
- *Optional:* Personal Journal (Follow Mindful Journaling style of writing)

Learning and Teaching Approach

Knowledge emerges only through invention and reinvention, through the restless, impatient, continuing, hopeful inquiry human beings pursue in the world, with the world, and with each other.

Paulo Freire[1]

This book mainly focuses on introducing concepts that students can understand by answering reflective questions each week. This process is inspired by Paulo Freire's approach to teaching through inquiry. This inquiry process can help the reader identify areas of work, negative habits, and behaviors so they can start replacing them with new culturally attuned perspectives, habits, and behaviors.

To foster mindfulness from the author's angle, all the content, concepts, and written language - especially the design of the reflective questions, choice of words, illustrations, quotes, proverbs, and phrases - have been designed to establish an affective-caring environment.

Also, to add more cultural sensitivity, the participants will find throughout the guide traditional Latinx proverbs and sayings (*dichos*) with a translation. It is intended as a small break of reflection from all the new concepts presented, and perhaps connect with others to reflect as a group. Also, because… "Proverbs are rich wisdom present in all cultures. They are saying used to pass on values and to teach children about life – what is wrong and what is right. Often proverbs show people how to be successful in life" (Juana Bordas[2]).

Week 1

How Are You?

Week 1 - How Are You?

This week we will work together in investigating what is happening inside of us, mostly in our heads – what do I mean? I am referring to that voice that is always with us, even as you read this…notice the internal dialogue, thoughts, comments, and/or judgments – can you notice it? In this first section, we will learn more about our inner world, including this voice. I will start by sharing with you my personal experience with my inner world. After years of self-work and therapy, I came to understand that my voice was a highly impatient-worrisome-ruminating voice, and after years of neglecting any type of mental health care routine led me to experience generalized anxiety.

In 2011, I found myself in an ambulance gasping for air, unable to control my shaking body and feeling my heart wanting to jump out of my chest, so fast-paced I thought I had a heart attack. I was not dying. I was experiencing an anxiety attack[1]. How did I get to this place mentally and physically? As I got closer to my thirties, the life that I had planned, my "American Dream" was not even close to becoming a reality. Failed intimate relationships, career blocks, and the pressures to meet the expectations of society for women and Latinx women were eating me alive. I had moved to a new country of opportunity, but I was not getting the opportunities I dreamed of. This new place made me feel like I didn't belong. (This is one of the biggest struggles of Latinx Immigrants – and we will work on this through this guidebook).

This guide-book gathers a lot of the knowledge I have gained in the past seven years of healing and loving myself. I hope that after you finish this chapter, you are able to connect and understand a little better

21

what happens inside of you and how to start caring for yourself so you can find that place of belonging within you.

Please take a small break to think and reflect on this *Dicho.* Consider how you feel at this moment.

> ## "Nadie sabe lo que hay en la olla más que la cuchara que la menea"
>
> Translation: Nobody knows what is inside the pot, only the spoon that is mixing it. [a]

Mental Health and the Mind

When the mind reigns in peace, it is always happy, although the external conditions are far from being the most favorable. The body can have means to be healthy, but if the mind does not enjoy peace, it is impossible to be happy, even if it was surrounded by the best conditions.

Dalai Lama[1]

Let's start this process of belonging and giving birth to new perspectives (Pertenæcer) by understanding mental health, our minds, and what happens inside our heads and triggers down to our bodies. Dr. Daniel Siegel defines subjective experience as what happens inside of us. Subjective experience is the feeling of emotion, the texture of thought, the beliefs we have, the perceptions we hold, the intentions that go through us, the meanings embedded in our narratives[4].

Before my incident (anxiety attack or *Ataque de nervios* as it is known in most Latin countries) from the last section, these were foreign words to me and foreign concepts I was not interested in learning or knowing about. I felt that these were things only for crazy people (*locos*). Deep inside I carried many stigmas and barriers that kept me "safe," kept me from reaching out, kept me from learning healthy tools to cope with life's struggles, and kept me away from those with mental illnesses and disorders. Little did I know that mental illnesses are extremely common and that I was suffering from one of them: generalized anxiety disorder (You feel excessive, unrealistic worry and tension with little or no reason)[2]. So, why am I talking about anxiety and "crazy" people in a book about belonging? Because based on research, and from my own experience, people who do not have healthy tools to cope with life circumstances tied to migration can develop what is called Acculturative Stress[3], and ultimately if no healthy coping tools are applied, Latinx can develop mental health illnesses, like depression and anxiety - as it happened to me.

When I started experiencing anxiety attacks, I was not aware of my subjective experience. I didn't know that my heart, my brain, and mind had been in need of care for a long time. The first couple of years after moving to the United States, I understood (subtly and innocently) that my parents were scarifying a lot for me, and that I needed to succeed and attain the 'American Dream' so I could somehow pay them back. Mental hygiene or care was not part of my vocabulary or part of my priorities. The only way I knew how to cope with feeling overwhelmed or lost was by going out, partying, drinking, and just overall engaging in self-destructive behaviors.

It is not an easy process to befriend our subjective experience, however, for me, it has been worth every minute and second of my time. Perhaps now is the time for you! Congrats my friend for embarking on this journey – you are deserving of your own love and affection, and you belong everywhere and anywhere!

Take time to reflect on this *Dicho* and how it relates to your current or future mental health hygiene practices.

> ## "No hay mal que dure cien años ni cuerpo que lo resista"
>
> Translation: There is no harm that will last one hundred years and no body that can resist it. [a]

Mental Hygiene

Mental hygiene can be defined as the time dedicated to develop and maintain strong social support, as well as the cultivation of purpose, perspective, and humor in one's life[4]. In other words, the act of getting to know your internal world, and identifying harmful mental habits and patterns that create the imbalance in our lives, therefore devoting time to cultivate healthy tools, habits, and patterns.

In this guidebook, we will learn how to care for our Mental Health by learning mental hygiene practices through the practice of reflection, mindfulness practices, and guided meditation exercises. These tools can help decrease stress and bring balance, ease, and understanding of our individual subjective experiences, as it does to me in my daily life. Committed practice and care can allow us to be mentally fit so we can flourish in life and work with and through the hardships of life as an immigrant.

Mental Health in the Latinx Immigrant Community

According to reviewed research for this book, there is a need to address low rates of participation in mental health care from the Latinx community in the United States. Some of the reasons for low engagement and participation[1] are:

- Our help-seeking attitudes
- Mental health stigmas
- Environmental constraints
- Affordability of services
- Symptoms of distress

Personally, I can attest to this because I faced all of these reasons. First I needed to overcome the barrier that I needed help, second the fear of learning about mental health, and lastly the stigmas to attend therapy. It took a lot of strength to overcome the shame and feeling of personal responsibility that I had let this happen to myself. The fear of being judged by those who I loved was a big one too; it took me almost two years after my episode in the ambulance for me to accept that self-help books and positivism were not working for me and my wellbeing.

Based on research, the common traits that lead Latinxs into success in the United States involve the ability to smoothly navigate the mainstream U.S. culture as well as their growing and changing ethnic-cultural enclaves, in other words, the ability to negotiate between these different cultural contexts successfully. Acculturated Latinxs show that they have a set of skills that promote effective adaptation[2]. Therefore, achieving the American dream involves the ability to create a sense of belonging here and there.

Take time to reflect on this *Dicho* and how it related to your journey as an immigrant.

"Poco a poco se llega lejos"
Translation: Little by little one goes further.[a]

REFLECTIVE QUESTIONS:

- What is the American Dream for you?

Ser libre, feliz, sentir que pertenezce
tener accese a servicias y beneficios

- Do you pressure yourself to attain this dream? If so, what unhealthy habits can you identify in your day-to-day life?

Mi alimentaGion

- Does this American Dream feel attainable? If no, why?

It does mera now than
before.

- Would this dream give you a sense of fulfillment? If yes, how? If no, why?

Si, me haría sentir que tengo
derechos y que puedo alcanzer mis
metas en este país.

- What expectations are you putting onto yourself that are not realistic?

- Have you felt like you don't belong? If yes, what do you feel?

Si muchas veces, siento que
no me entienden, que no encajo o
que no sé que está pasando.

- Think of a group, place or circumstance where you want to belong. Why do you want to belong here?

Ciertos Grupos de americanos, quiero integrarme mas. Quiero pertenecer porque sen personas importantes para mi esposo.

- What is keeping you from feeling like you don't belong in this group, place or circumstance?

Parte el idioma, acento, chistes internos e Temas culturales.

What is Stress?

If you ask anyone in my family about me as a child, they will say that I cried a lot. I don't recall being a crying baby and little girl, but most sources confirm that I was! Why am I telling you this? Because stress is manifested in many ways during our lives. Many people naturally develop tools to cope with change, aversion, and fear, but others, like me, do not naturally develop or have those tools.

The Stress Management Society explains stress as primarily a physical response. When we are stressed, our body thinks we are under attack and immediately switches to a mode called "fight or flight", they also added a third mode which is the "freeze" mode. What happens? Our bodies start releasing a mix of hormones and chemicals to prepare our bodies into physical action, all depending on which of the three modes is our default mode. Each mode causes several reactions that will be explored later in this chapter. For now, it is important to know that the "fight or flight" has been part of the human existence for thousands of years, this mode helped us survive dangerous situations, and today it still helps us survive and evade danger. The challenge is when our body goes into a state of stress in inappropriate situations[1]. As it started to happen to me when I was experiencing anxiety attacks and generalized anxiety.

What is the flight or fight or Freeze mode?

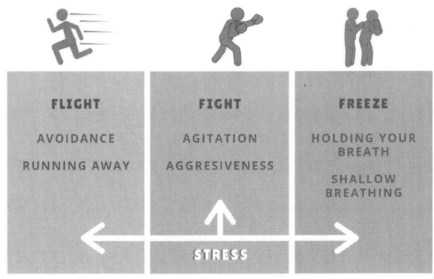

Source: See notes[1]

This image describes what happens in each of us when we are under stress. It can manifest in us in three ways. First, it can be a feeling of avoidance or trying to flee or leave the situation. The second one is agitation, annoyance, and aggressive behavior towards others. Lastly, it can also manifest in our breathing by either becoming uptight and holding our breath or in short and shallow breathing that naturally will require us to take deep breaths to prevent hyperventilation.

For example, when I used to ride crowded public transportation (I am now able to notice), my default response was the Flight mode. For me, it manifested with the sensation of wanting to get off and leave. In others, it may manifest with rudeness through pushing or being rude to other riders, or just the shallow and rapid breathing and bodily discomfort. This week the mindfulness practice will help us start identifying our default stress, and slowly identify our triggers and reactions - take time to practice throughout the week.

How does stress manifest in our bodies?

As we have learned, stress can manifest in many ways; for me as a child, it manifested through the fight mode: moaning and crying. As an adult, it started to manifest through the flight mode, with racing thoughts, body aches, digestion problems, acne, cold sores, rapid heartbeat, sweatiness, impatience, unsettledness, fidgeting, etc. And after many years of not having healthy tools to cope with stress, I developed generalized anxiety disorder[1]. Please note that the chronic and damaging behaviors and thoughts that we all have is not something that we do consciously or do on purpose. Through the introduction of new mindfulness and meditative practices, we will learn how to identify and try to change these negative patterns caused by stress. This process will require your commitment to learning openly and the will to live a better life. If I have been able to manage stress, anxiety, and feelings of not belonging, you can do that and many more things as well!

Constant and prolonged stress can manifest in many ways. Research has identified the following bodily effects:[2]

- Back pain
- Muscular tension, aches, and disorders
- Fatigue
- Cardiovascular problems
- Digestive problems
- Immunological problems
- Reproductive system problems
- Mental health disorders

Prolonged stress that becomes chronic and persistent increases the chances of developing mental health disorders, as listed above. This graphic can give you a sense of what can happen if there is chronic anger, fear, and sadness.

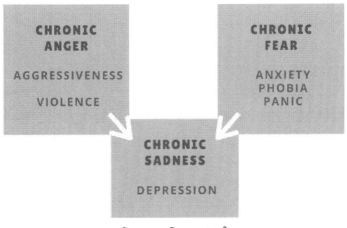

Source: See notes[2]

Chronic fear can subsequently manifest into anxiety – as it happened to me. My thoughts and mind were unconsciously focused on fear, and the prolonged exposure to these states of mind without any type of mental health hygiene led me to develop Generalized Anxiety Disorder. I don't want to instill fear in you. Instead, I want you to be aware of the effects of living a life without mental hygiene.

What is acculturative stress?

In 1996, a study measured the acculturation stress levels of Hispanic college students in the United States. It was highlighted that acculturative stress originated from the difficulties in communicating and understanding the English language, plus difficulties with fitting in or feeling that they belong. It became evident that these conditions aggravated feelings of loneliness and alienation for late-immigrant Hispanic students[1]. Another article in 2012 reviewed the effects of immigration and the inability to adapt to the dominant culture by identifying acculturative stressors. The identified traits were pressures of learning a new language, balancing differing cultural values, and having to negotiate between American and Latino ways of daily living[2].

I can personally attest to experiencing these symptoms of acculturative stress – can you? Being an immigrant exposed me to the stressors of not being able to connect with others because of the language barrier (something that was frustrating and isolating), the feeling of being misunderstood and not fitting in with my peers (something that was stressful and painful). Slowly, I learned that I was different and perhaps that I belonged somewhere else, but I was not sure where...Thankfully, I was able to meet other teenagers going through a similar experience, and it was helpful – how has it been for you?

After years of learning about self-love and care, I came to realize that true belonging can only originate from accepting and embracing our unique selves. There is no need for a physical place, it is always inside of us, in this subjective experience. Therefore, this week we will start working with befriending our internal world (subjective experience), so we can find this place of belonging and eventually see that we belong everywhere and anywhere.

Take a break to reflect on this *Dicho,* based it on your life as an immigrant and this journey.

> ## "El que a buen árbol se arrima, buena sombra le cobija"
>
> Translation: One that seeks a good tree, will be covered by a good shade. [a]

Why train the Mind?

> My mind is like a puppy,
> it likes to wander and explore.
> If I don't watch it carefully
> it goes through any open door.
>
> Andrew Jordan Nance

Not knowing how to manage my internal world is what triggered anxiety, and stress in my life, and it was the main reason I started to try to understand what people meant when they said, "you need to tame and be the ruler of your mind and body." I had no idea what they meant! I just knew that I felt like I was not in control and/or losing control of my head, my body, my emotions, and my life. I was the passenger of my life, not the driver.

As Latinxs immigrants, we face the stresses of everyday life along with the stresses of being an immigrant. It is extremely important that we teach our minds to be our friends, our bodies to be our allies, and our hearts to connect to love, compassion, and empathy.

REFLECTIVE QUESTIONS:

- What experiences, circumstances or scenarios are stressful for you?

- What experiences trigger stress in you?

_____

_____

_____

_____

_____

- How do you feel physically, mentally, and emotionally when you are stressed?

_____

_____

_____

_____

_____

- How do you manage the stress of being an immigrant?

_____

_____

_____

_____

_____

_____

- From the things you have learned about immigrants, which symptoms of acculturative stress do you relate to? And how?

_____

_____

_____

_____

_____

- Do you think other family members or your parents suffer from acculturative stress? If yes, describe who and what is happening to them.

_____

_____

_____

- Do you feel in control of your mind, your emotions and your body? If yes or no, explain how you feel.

_____

_____

_____

_____

_____

- What can you change in your daily routine to find mental, emotional, and physical balance?

- What are some tools you use to cope with the stress of being an immigrant?

The Power of Breath

My breath has become my home, my safe place, my sanctuary – that sounds cheesy, but it's true! All my life, before learning about meditation and mindfulness, I used to cope with stress with unhealthy habits, and habits that brought peace from outside and not from within. You probably know what I am talking about…As humans, we do all unhealthy things to numb the pain and/or avoid confronting it. When I learned to connect with my breath in a meaningful way, my life changed! Our breath can bring us instantly to the present moment, try it now, take a deep breath! How does it feel? Good – right? That is the power of your breath. The guided meditation this week will revolve around connecting healthily with our breath.

MINDFULNESS ACTIVITY:

My Breath is My Home

In this exercise, we will learn how our breath changes as we bring to mind three (3) scenarios that bring stress to you in your life. At the end of the exercise, I invite you to do the guided meditation so you can bring yourself back to center and tranquility.

- ☐ Level 1 – Think of something small like noticing that someone parked in your parking spot, or that there is no hot water to shower, etc…
- ☐ Level 2 – Think of something that is manageable but a little more stressful like being stuck in traffic, running late for a meeting or an appointment, etc…
- ☐ Level 3 – Think of something that is a little harder to manage such as hearing that you will lose your job, getting news that you or a loved one is diagnosed with a life-threatening disease, etc…

MEDITATION PRACTICE:

Solo Respira (Breathing Meditation)

- Length: 5 minutes
- Practice five (5) times this week.

The power of your breath has the power to transform your present life into a haven. This guided meditation will introduce tips on how to meditate with your breath.

For guided meditation, go to www.almayespiritu.com/guidedmeditations

Password to access: pertenæcer

Week 2

Connecting with My Story, My Ancestors, and

My Culture

Week 2 – Connecting with My Story, My Ancestors, and My Culture

"Caminante, no hay camino, se hace camino al andar"
Translation: Walker there is no path, the path is made by walking.
Antonio Machado

In the process of healing ourselves from the anxieties and stressors of being immigrants, I have learned that we must first reconnect with who we are and where we come from. As explained in the last section, some of the factors tied to acculturative stress[1] are:

- Immigration circumstances
- Balancing and negotiating different cultural values
- Learning a new language
- Battling feelings of isolation and not belonging

Immigration Circumstances

This week I want you to take some time to reflect on your Immigration circumstances. For example, in my own story, the decision to migrate was made by my parents; therefore, my migration circumstance was involuntary. I was not even born when my parents applied for a family visa into the United States; and in 1998, my parents got the news that we had been approved to reside legally in the US. At the time, Venezuela was starting to go through some economic, social, and political turmoil; it became more and more common to hear of people getting robbed, kidnapped, or assaulted. Job opportunities for young professionals, like my future self, were rare and rarer for women. Being underpaid, overworked, and oppressed were everyday experiences for young professionals in Venezuela. It was common to see protesters out on the streets on a weekly basis; being in fear was a common way to live. Even though Venezuela was a rich country, my parents, my sisters, and I could see how it was starting to crumble, and there was very little that we could do; my future and the future of my sisters seemed very unclear and unstable. Even though I was not old enough to make the decision, the decision was made for me. It took years for me to understand and come to terms with the fact that it was the best decision my parents could have made. I now own this decision as if it were my own – how was it for you? Did you make the decision? Did your parents or family members make that decision for you? Was the decision based on the search for civil rights, educational opportunities, family safety, etc.? The important part here is to know our story, because as author Juana Bordas[1] states in her book *Salsa, Soul and Spirit*, "Our stories are a collective journey, small streams forming a powerful river, a dynamic force that is restructuring our country into a multicultural society". When we know our story, and we share it, we empower ourselves and others, and in the process, we come to embrace and accept who we are, where we are, and why we are here. Answering these questions and the exercise of narrating our story will be part of your journal writing assignment this week.

REFLECTIVE QUESTIONS:

- Tell your migration story. You may write it over and over until you feel confident that this story truly shows the meaning behind the decision. Was it your decision? Or did your parents or family members make that decision for you? Was the decision based on the search for civil rights, educational opportunities, family safety, etc.?

_____

_____

_____

_____

_____

- Who in your family can help you learn more about your heritage and family traditions? How can you reconnect or connect with them?

_____

_____

_____

_____

_____

- What would you want to learn about your ancestry and heritage?

- What family traditions have you continued to practice after leaving your home country?

Balancing and Negotiating Cultural Values

Now let's reflect on balancing different cultural values and having to negotiate between the American and Latino ways of daily living. As you may or may not already know, the Latinx culture is considered a highly collectivist society, and the American culture is regarded as a highly individualistic society[1]. Hence, stress can be generated in us when trying to navigate in individualistic communities with a collectivistic mindset or vice versa. Not all Latin American cultures are fully collective cultures; there can be some with high individualistic influences. It can vary in the diversity of Latin American cultures. This week take some time to reflect on the individualistic and collectivist culture at home, your community, your home country, and the United States. Please note, that this is something I recently learned, and it made complete sense to me! Maybe it will or will not to you, just take the time to reflect.

What is a collectivist culture?

In this type of society, the core unit is the group. There is a sense of belonging togetherness. Individuals are seen as fundamentally connected and related through relationships[1]. One trait that is common in collectivist cultures is *familismo*[2], which refers to how Latinos tend to be highly group-oriented. The opinion of the family is very important. Therefore, there is a strong emphasis placed on the family as the major source of one's identity and protection against the hardships of life.

Soon after we immigrated, I started to experience a clash between these two cultures. It has taken years for my family and for me to embrace and accept that some aspects of life fall into the individualistic culture influence, and others under the collectivist culture mindset. One of the tools we can develop to ease the acculturative stress and stressors is being able to understand that there is no need to lose our identity and cultural values so we can fit in. There can be conscious adaptations made, but it is extremely important to understand where we come from and where we are regarding culture. Hence, in collectivist cultures, there is still an individual, but this individual exists as it relates to others[3].

What is an individualistic culture?

In this type of culture, risk and change are embraced. Self-identity and self-interest are the main drivers. The individual needs overtake the collective ones, although not in a selfish way; instead, it is a sign of maturity and a form of serving society through living up to the individual's potential. Individualistic cultures are based on competition, and getting things done is an essential and admirable skill in individualistic cultures[4]. The decisions I made up until my late twenties were based on what my family thought was best for me; this was draining and exhausting to my soul and my body. Guilt and shame were always present, as family members were also battling between the importance of family, and the importance of living your individual goals and dreams. With time, I learned to slowly find a good balance of family opinion and my own. The acculturation process is not about forgetting what is important to you; it is about learning how to balance and negotiate between your native and new cultures.

At times, acculturative stress leads us to make decisions based out of fear of rejection, fear of being judged, and fear of being isolated. Please take some time to reflect on the root of your decisions, and the power you give to those around you.

REFLECTIVE QUESTIONS:

- How would you define your culture? Highly collective? Half and a half? Highly Individualistic? In another way?

- How do you manage the influence of your family on your decisions?

- How much control do you have over your life and your life's decisions?

- When considering family opinions do you base your decisions on fear from them or out love for them?

_____

_____

_____

_____

_____

- How can you find balance in using collectivist mindset and the individualistic view without hurting yourself or your loved ones?

_____

_____

_____

_____

_____

Learning a New Language

If you are reading this book, you have been able to overcome the biggest stressor for Latinx immigrants – learning a new language, so congratulations!!

However, there is one of thing that still lingers in me, and may in you as well. It is the discomfort and stress generated by speaking with an accent in white-dominant environments. The first hurdle in learning a new language was probably losing the fear to speak – right? The second obstacle for me, and may have been for you too, was being able to be understood and pronouncing things in a way that others could understand me. Thirdly, like me, you probably had to overcome the fear of building friendships and social circles in this second language. So, as all foreign language immigrants know, it is not an easy process to learn a new language. And as we overcome these hurdles, other ones appear on the road. I'm not sure what stressors you may be experiencing now, but hopefully, this guidebook has touched on some of these, and I hope that together we can work on diminishing some of these obstacles. How? By working with embracing ourselves, our uniqueness, our roots, our culture, and our ancestry. I have learned in these past few years that knowledge can help us heal ourselves and heal others.

Did you know that back in the 1600s when people immigrated to America from Europe, they were urged to cut ties with their homelands, to forget their customs and language, and join the melting pot?[1] ...This is no longer the case! See the Oath that immigrants[2] below, this oath is taken at the naturalization ceremony, like me, you may have arrived at this point, or may soon arrive. I included here because I want to remind you of what the United States when asks of us when becoming a US citizen,

> "I hereby declare, on oath, that I absolutely and entirely renounce and abjure all allegiance and fidelity to any foreign prince, potentate, state, or sovereignty, of whom or which I have heretofore been a subject or citizen; that I will support and defend the Constitution and laws of the United States of America against all enemies, foreign and domestic; that I will bear true faith and allegiance to the same; that I will bear arms on behalf of the United States when required by the law; that I will perform noncombatant service in the Armed Forces of the United States when required by the law; that I will perform work of national

importance under civilian direction when required by the law; and that I take this obligation freely, without any mental reservation or purpose of evasion; so help me God."

Did you see that no statements are asking us to renounce our traditions, our language, or our heritage? These are aspects that are personal to each of us, that make us unique – our accent is the stamp of our uniqueness, of our history, and of our heritage. Please take some time to think about this and the questions in the reflective section.

REFLECTIVE QUESTIONS:

- How do you differentiate your accent from others?

- What makes your accent unique? (Think about your native tongue and how some of the phonetics transfer beautifully to the English language).

Battling Feelings of Isolation and Not Belonging

Once we belong thoughtfully to ourselves and believe thoughtfully in ourselves, true belonging is ours. Belonging to ourselves means being called to stand alone – to brave the wilderness of uncertainty, vulnerability, and criticism.

Brené Brown[1]

Leaving the best for last! One of the most difficult parts of being an immigrant is working through or experiencing these feelings of loneliness and not belonging[2]. I'm in my mid-thirties now, and recently I became an immigrant in a new country, Spain. In a way, I am grateful to be in this position because it is helping me reconnect with the process of acculturation and adaptation. As a young Latina, I recall this urge to connect and build friendships. It was hard enough to be exposed to a new culture that I didn't understand and then trying to learn a new language, but on top of that, it is this difficult feeling of being an outcast. The way I looked, the way I dressed, the way I talked, the way I moved, the way I thought friendship or relationships worked all of a sudden was weird and different. Have you have ever felt, imagined or experienced anything like this? Well, you are not alone!

John Cacioppo[3] describes loneliness as perceived social isolation when we feel disconnected. Brené Brown explains that loneliness is very different than being alone because at the heart of loneliness is the absence of meaningful social interaction – an intimate relationship, friendships, family gatherings, or even community or group connections; being alone, instead of seen as the act of solitude can be a powerful healing tool.[3] Sometimes these connections we are yearning for can take form in many ways, such as talking to a stranger at the dentist's office while you wait and sharing your common dread of having your mouth examined and cleaned; or it can be a Skype call with a loving friend or family member, both of these are personal samples.

Through meditation, mindfulness, and reflection in this guidebook we are learning to know ourselves, our triggers to stress, and our needs – such as the need to find deep connections, which manifests as feelings of loneliness. Remember, it is not the number of connections, but the quality of these connections that matter. Take time to practice the mindful connection activity from the mindfulness practices this week.

Take a break to reflect on this *Dicho* and how it can be applied to this feeling of loneliness in a new country.

"Mi Casa es tu Casa"

TTranslation: My home is your home. [a]

REFLECTIVE QUESTIONS:

- What is the difference between being alone and feeling lonely?

_____

_____

_____

_____

- Being an immigrant is not easy, when have you felt the loneliest?

_____

_____

_____

_____

- What thoughts could you identify that appear when you feel lonely?

- Do you think there are others that feel lonely and isolated because they are immigrants? If so, how can you connect with them?

- What can you change in your perspective to feel like you belong?

- When was the last time you felt connected and felt like you belonged? Describe the situation and what you felt (mentally and physically).

_____

_____

_____

_____

_____

- How could you re-live that moment in the best possible way without having to leave (physically) the place where you are now?

_____

_____

_____

_____

_____

MINDFULNESS ACTIVITIES:

1. Ancestral Greeting[1]

This exercise gives us a sense of connection and understanding of our ancestry and lineage. It connects us with the wisdom, guidance, and energy from our roots.

☐ Speak out loud the following phrases, if you do not know the names of your ancestors, dedicate some time to investigate. If this is not a possibility, practice with those who you consider your family and its ancestry.

I am _____ the daughter/son/child of

_____ and _____, the great

grandson/granddaughter/grandchild of_____ and

_____, _____ and

_____, the great-grandson/great-

granddaughter/great-grandchild of _____ and

_____, _____ and _____, the great-

great grandson/great-great granddaughter/great-great grandchild

of _____ and _____, _____ and

_____.

☐ Write in your journal about the feelings experienced while connecting with your past and your roots in this way. Did you experience the power of ancestry?

2. Mindful Connection

This exercise will involve a two-minute meditation (Identifying Loneliness) to identify feelings of loneliness and need for connection. If the need is identified, please follow the steps below.

- ☐ If you were able to identify the need for meaningful connection. Please take time to identify 2-3 people that may be available to connect.
- ☐ Ask yourself: is this person going to nourish my wellbeing or detract from it?
  - ☐ Does our usual conversation leave me with a sense of tranquility and enthusiasm?
  - ☐ Or does it leave me with a sense of depletion and unsettledness?
- ☐ Choose a person that nourishes your well-being, however, do not create expectations
- ☐ Reach out and set a time to meet in person
  - ☐ If an in-person meeting is not possible, give them a call or schedule a video call
- ☐ Do not plan the topics to discuss, let the conversation flow
- ☐ During the meeting/call try not to have distractions around, practice being present and listening deeply

MEDITATION PRACTICES:

1. Identifying Loneliness (Two-Minute meditation)
- Length: 2 minutes
- Practice as needed

This meditation can help you identify feelings of loneliness or that need to connect meaningfully with others. It will help you define loneliness versus alone time.

2. My accent is my unique stamp in the world (Self-Compassion Meditation)

- Length: 10 minutes
- Practice five (5) times this week

Our accent is the stamp of our uniqueness, of our history, and of our heritage. This meditation will work with embracing, accepting, and loving the way we sound and speak in the world.

Optional: Practice twice (2) this week Self-Timed Silent Breathing Meditation (no audio).

For guided meditation, go to www.almayespiritu.com/guidedmeditations

Password to access: pertenæcer

Week 3

Embracing a New Perspective

Week 3 – Embracing a New Perspective

This week we will learn the definitions of mindfulness and meditation, as well as the benefits of mindfulness and meditation practices, plus mindfulness as a mental hygiene tool. Why learn this new alternative way of care? Because it worked and still works for me, and I am sure that it can work for you, just try it! - I know that I will use these tools for the rest of my life! Would you?

The day I opened to new ways of seeing, being, and behaving I was able to see the amazing changes in me. They were not immediate changes; it took time, but it felt right. It all started during my therapy sessions when I learned about *vinyasa* yoga. *Vinyasa* is a very subtle, beautiful, introspective practice, and exercise can be a side benefit. Yoga specifically is about getting to know yourself better and learning how to love yourself[1]. After listening to the advice of my therapist, I started to practice *vinyasa* yoga at home through online videos. It was not comfortable to sit steadily, and more to connect with my body and my breath. I felt the urge to move, do something else, and just run away from this slow motion and introspective work. However, the time allowed me to find that peace and calmness soon followed these feelings of discomfort and uneasy. I learned that the tranquility and comfort I found in slowing down were priceless - So please do not let that or anything stop you!

Even today there are days where I struggle to get settled in yoga or in any bodily practice; eventually, I start to enjoy the movements and the connection with my body. In the past, body movement for me involved competitive or purposeful exercise; in other words, either I was training for competition or training to get in shape – it was never about finding peace or working on my wellbeing. This has completely changed, and I am a better competitor because of that; relaxing and not thinking about winning has allowed me to perform better.

Soon after I started to learn *Vinyasa* Yoga, my therapist began to guide me through short meditations during my sessions. I allowed myself to trust and follow, and I will never regret that – So please allow yourself at this time to trust and practice the weekly guided meditations, even if discomfort is present. If you try them for a while and you don't enjoy them, then choose something else. But all I am asking you is to allow this new alternative way of care to enter your life, test it, and prove for yourself if it works or not. Personally, these practices allow me to relieve stress and manage my anxiety. As a last note, *Vinyasa* yoga was my stepping stone into the world of mindfulness; mindfulness practices and concepts have become essential tools in my day-to-day life – and as you can see, it also became my vocation to share these tools!

What is Mindfulness?

It took a long time for me to actually understand what Jon Kabat-Zinn[1] describes as mindfulness. He explains that it is the moment-to-moment, non-judgmental awareness, cultivated by paying attention in a specific way, that is, in the present moment, and as non-reactively, as non-judgmental, and as open-heartedly as possible. What does this really mean? For me, in a way it meant that calmness we see underwater. Sometimes the ocean can be stirred up, but underneath the surface, there is always tranquility. I read about mindfulness, but I still didn't know how to get to this place of calmness and tranquility…I just knew that there had to be another way that I could live and not be pulled and run over by my own emotions and thoughts.

As time passed, I came to understand that mindfulness also meant that I was like the sky and the weather. How so? Well, there are storms and weathers (thoughts and emotions) that pass along the sky (me), and I have the choice to observe and let the weather pass by without judgment or reactions, and with just humble acceptance, like the stillness of the blue sky. It may or may not be easy for you to see this now, but I promise you that with time and dedication you will be able to see how you can be in control of those weathers passing through you.

Another way to understand mindfulness is, as a way to promote positive mental health and adaptation by interrupting rambling thoughts that give rise to suffering[2]. So, in this process, we learn to pay attention to that voice in our heads and see if it's good or damaging to us. If it is damaging chatter, it is probably creating stress, anxiety, and worries in our lives. Please know that I was not always aware of that voice in my head, and you probably aren't either... It is automatic and nonstop. So why bother to mess with it? Because if we let this voice get out of our control and run our lives, we most likely will end up living our lives through fear, sadness, or anger (we will learn more about these emotions in week five).

What is a Mindfulness Practice?

In mindfulness practices, we exercise acceptance of mental states, emotions, and body; also, we work with training the mind to focus and see clearly without the noise of overwhelming thoughts, worries, plans, daydreaming, etc. In other words, we become aware of the mental, emotional and physical sensations and happenings that manifest in our mental, physical, emotional states. It is our role to become the observer, and become aware and embracive of whatever state is present in the body, mind, and heart. By practicing relaxation from this place of observation and insight, we can introduce new wholesome ways of relating to negative and uncomfortable states of mind, body, and heart.[1]

Mindfulness trains two important faculties: attention and meta-attention. Attention is something we all understand. Attention is taking possession by the mind, in clear and vivid form, and meta-attention is the ability to know that your attention has wandered away. [2]

Get it? Just in case you are like me, here is a simplified explanation: mindfulness practice is basically finding a place of stillness that allows us to not let our thoughts or our emotions become the frontrunners of your life. We learn to know when we are on autopilot (unaware) and when we are present (aware). We become the master and ruler of our mind, body, and heart.

REFLECTIVE QUESTIONS:

- What can you do (mentally and physically) to open and allow yourself to embrace a new perspective and an alternative form of care?

- Does mindfulness sound like something you can do? If so, when will be the best time to practice and where?

- Think about a time that you a felt that sensation of pure presence. How did it feel physically? Mentally? And Emotionally?

What is Meditation?

For years, I thought meditation was just sitting there and trying to clear my mind – have no thoughts! In case you have not tried…that is impossible! The mind is always on and cannot be turned off. Instead in meditation, we learn to train the mind to be our best friend and ally; even more, we learn to be in control of it.

There are many types of meditations, but to get an overall understanding. Meditation can be defined as the practice intended to train our mind to pay attention so we can be more aware and conscious of our internal world, surroundings, and the present moment[1]. In this guidebook, we will learn these types of meditations:

- Breathing Meditation (Week 1 and 2)
- Self-acceptance Meditation (Week 2)
- Mindfulness of body Meditation (Week 3)
- Self-regulation Meditation (Week 4)
- Self-Compassion and Compassion Meditation (Week 5 and 6)
- Insight Meditation (Week 7 and 8)

It is important for you to also know what meditation is not, this helped me a lot because it answered a lot of my doubts.

WHAT MEDITATION IS NOT...

- A RELIGION
- A SPECIAL SKILL
- A PRACTICE THAT REQUIRES A SPECIAL PREPARATION
- SOMETHING THAT REQUIRES A LOT OF YOUR TIME
- A WAY TO ELIMINATE SORROW OR BAD MOMENTS
- AN ATTEMPT TO STOP THINKING
- INSISTING ONLY ON POSITIVE THOUGHTS
- SOMETHING THAT ASKS YOU TO RENUNCE PERSONAL OPINIONS, OBJECTIVES OR PASSIONS
- COMMAND TO STOP HAVING FUN

Source: See notes[2]

As I shared with you earlier my first formal experience with mindfulness and meditation was with *Vipassana* or 'insight' meditation. In this type of meditation, one is learning to focus attention on the breath while simply observing any sensations, thoughts, or feelings that arise[3]. I also mentioned that the first time I formally meditated was in therapy. I recall lying on my therapist's couch, while she started to guide me to pay attention to my breath. It was the most difficult thing I had ever experienced. I had no idea how to pay attention to my body or my breath! It will most likely be way easier for you, it was harder for me because my anxiety levels were high; in other words, fear was deeply embedded in my psyche, mind, and heart. If it is hard, that's ok too! Just try to relax and trust it will get better.

Also, note that meditation can be practiced through mindfulness as a type of awareness of the different things happening in our subjective and bodily experience, these both are well-connected and intertwined.

We will learn how to do this as I introduce more weekly meditations throughout the guidebook.

Benefits of Mindfulness and Meditation

Are you asking yourself, "Why meditate? What am I getting from this?"? Here are some of the self-proven benefits of mindfulness and meditation; some of them are also scientifically[1] proven! Try it for yourself, if it works – as it did for me, keep doing it! If not, you know what to do.

- Have a coping tool that you can carry with you ANYWHERE!
- Increase self-knowledge and self-love
- Regain the lost energy of trying to control everything
- Build a good relationship with change
- Learn to be more present and aware
- Build your ability to focus
- More efficiency in the things you do at home and at work
- Fewer mistakes and conflict at home and at work
- Less stress-related body aches
- Better pain tolerance
- More compassion and empathy
- Increased awareness and concentration
- Emotion regulation
- Discovering new ways to cope more effectively with existing conditions difficulties, pain or suffering
- Learning to take better care of oneself

This guidebook doesn't guarantee or promise any of these or other results. Instead, it emphasizes engagement and critique from each reader and participant to experience for themselves whatever is happening and what benefits are becoming evident, rather than base them on what this guidebook or research tells them to feel, achieve or experience.

REFLECTIVE QUESTIONS:

- What are some chores and activities that you would consider meditative practices?

_____

_____

_____

_____

- How can you convert some of your daily activities and routines into meditation?

_____

_____

_____

_____

- List some of the benefits you have noticed since starting a meditation and mindfulness practice three weeks ago.

_____

_____

_____

_____

Mindfulness and Meditation as Mental Hygiene Tools

I hope that through the cultivation of new ways of relating to thoughts, you can learn to identify fatalistic patterns that may be keeping you from being relaxed and belonging to yourself like happened to me. In case you were not aware, Fatalism is very present in our Latinx cultures. So this week we will work on identifying the presence of fatalistic mindsets and patterns. But first, you might want to know what I mean about Fatalism for Latinx, right?

Fatalismo (fatalism) emphasizes the 'here and now' and tends to promote an external locus of control. The *dicho* (saying) El hombre propone y Dios dispone (Man proposes, and God disposes of) characterizes this value of relinquishing false notions of control. Fatalism is typically associated with religiosity or spirituality and involves individuals turning to, trusting in, and surrendering to God's will, a higher power, or external forces[1]. It is also seen as a strong belief that uncertainty is inherent in life and each day is taken as it comes and a belief that the individual can do little to alter fate[2]. Is this starting to sound familiar? For me it did. Somewhere ingrained in me was this belief that some things were meant to be regardless of my intervention. As research shows, Latinxs traditionally have had a strong sense of destiny and a belief in divine providence governing the world. Major life events are seen as inevitable, and there is a fatalistic attitude that whatever shall be, shall be.[3]

"El hombre propone y Dios dispone"

Translation: Man proposes and God disposesa. [a]

This may or not may be true or you, but it is good to take time to reflect on this, and the *Dicho* above. Try to see if there are areas in life that you can have more control over.

REFLECTIVE QUESTIONS:

- In mental hygiene, we are caring for internal selves. Do you think the practices you are learning can become a priority in your life? If so, what adjustments can you start making in your daily routine?

_____

_____

_____

_____

_____

- Did you relate to the fatalistic mindset or patterns? If so, what did you find relatable?

_____

_____

_____

_____

- How can you start applying mindfulness when fatalistic mindsets and thoughts arise?

Mindfulness of Body

As we learned above, in mindfulness practices we become aware of our mental, emotional and physical sensations. We become the observer and become aware and embracive of whatever state is present in our body, mind, and heart. In mindfulness of the body this week, I want you to practice being aware of your body while you are doing things. This can be easily done, by just remembering to sense your breathing or sense if there is tension in the body and releasing it. You can do it while reading this or when you are doing a chore like doing laundry or washing dishes, or just while walking or driving to work. It doesn't mean that you are distracted; instead, you will move your attention away from the head (thoughts) into your body (presence).

I am asking you to pay more attention to your physical body and sensations. Why? Because most of the time we spend in our heads! See this graphic bellow; it shows an estimate of how much of our conscience is focused in each area of our awareness. For me, this was pretty accurate before I started to do mental health hygiene practices.

TRIANGLE OF AWARENESS

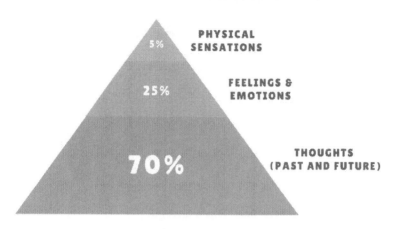

Source: See Notes[1]

REFLECTIVE QUESTIONS:

- What percentage would you give to each area of the triangle of conscience in your everyday life? Make sure it adds up to 100%.

Feelings and emotions	%
Physical sensations	%
Thoughts about the past and the future	%

- How do you feel about these percentages?

- What steps can you take to find balance and evenness in your everyday conscience?

- What activities can you choose to be more physically present?

- What are some activities that you already practice where you can be more alert and conscious?

MINDFULNESS ACTIVITIES:

1. Connecting with My Body

- ☐ Choose a physical activity that will allow you to get in touch with your body, for example:
    - ☐ Self-guided Dancing
    - ☐ Walking in nature
    - ☐ Running outdoors
    - ☐ *Vinyasa* Yoga
    - ☐ Tai-chi
    - ☐ Qigong
- ☐ Practice this activity twice (2) this week
- ☐ Be aware of your breath throughout the activity
- ☐ If distracted by pain or discomfort in the body, name the discomfort and then go back to the breath
    - ☐ Ex. Knee issues (Silently: *Knee pain-* and back to breath), Back issues (Silently: *Back pain -* and back to breath)

2. Mindful Cleansing

- ☐ This week make a choice to take 3 mindful showers or baths
    - ☐ Allow yourself to be present and not in a rush
    - ☐ Start by taking a deep breath as you enter the shower or bath
    - ☐ Once in the shower or bath:
        - Notice how the water feels in your body
        - Try to be aware of your thoughts and how they may distract you from being present
        - Do not fight your mind, instead, redirect your attention to sensing the water, the temperature, smelling the hair products or soaps, sensing how the water feels on your

skin, connect with the sensations and movements of cleaning yourself

- Do not get discouraged if the first couple of times, the mind translates you to the future or the past. This happens to me all the time! Just be kind to yourself, and once you realize that mind wandering – return to being present in the shower/bath

MEDITATION PRACTICE:

Aware of sensations, thoughts, and sounds (Mindfulness of body Meditation)
- Length: 10 minutes
- Practice five (5) times this week

This week's meditation will continue to be focused on breathing; however, we will work on overcoming and working with internal and external interruptions during practice.

Optional: Practice twice (2) this week Self-Timed Silent Breathing Meditation (no audio).
For guided meditation, go to www.almayespiritu.com/guidedmeditations
Password to access: pertenæcer

Week 4

Reigning the Mind and Body

Week 4 – Reigning the Mind and Body

This week, you will learn about mental health stigmas and its origins. Why? Because it is important to start to identify and understand if you may have some unidentified stigmas that are keeping you from fully engaging in mental health hygiene and self-care.

What is Mental Health Stigma?

Mental health stigma is a negative evaluation of those with mental illness or mental health treatment[1]. Stigmas are also defined as the internalization of stereotypes or discriminatory behavior toward others.

These negative experiences can be manifested through the actions and attitude of the practitioner treating the individual, his/her family members, and/or social influences[2]. These stigmas are deeply embedded in ourselves, our Latinx community, and our culture. These habitual actions and attitudes are hidden barriers that create resistance to embracing mental health care, treatment, and hygiene practices. Therefore, this process of reining our minds and bodies must include work at a personal, social, and cultural level.

Mental health stigmas can be very complicated; therefore, this guidebook uses two main categories: Family-community generated and self-generated. The Family-community generated stigmas include barriers generated from health providers, the system, the community, and our social network. Self-generated stigmas revolve around person-centered or personal belief-based stigmas[3].

How can you start identifying Family-Community generated and self-generated stigmas in your life? Please read and identify the statements below that apply to you.

Family-community Generated Mental Health Stigmas

The importance of family opinion and our role as community members can act as barriers preventing mental health participation and acceptance. Specifically, the effects of family, community, religion, access to health care, cultural competency barriers, and system generated barriers are the main obstacles within the family-community generated stigmas.

Please read along and identify in the next page the statements that apply to you. There is no wrong answer!

CHECK THE ONES THAT APPLY[4]

☐ In distress, I only reach out to people in my comfort zone (family, clergy)

☐ I find reaching outside of my comfort zone shameful to my family and me

☐ I am afraid to bring shame to my family if I engage in mental health hygiene

☐ I use communion at church as a safe place to express my distress and practice mental health hygiene

☐ My religious affiliation has a strong effect on the decision-making process for my family and me to practice mental health hygiene

☐ I believe that my distress comes from stronger forces outside of me and my control

☐ I attribute psychological distress to supernatural forces

☐ Everything occurs because of God's will, and it is ultimately out of my control

☐ I rather seek help with *curanderos* (Folk-healer) and *espiritualistas* (Spiritualists) or alternative sources of support

☐ It is more culturally accepted and less stigmatized to seek alternative care instead of practicing mental health hygiene

☐ (*Only women*) I am expected to maintain characteristics like the Virgin Mary, such as being selfless, unadulterated, docile, and coy

☐ I distrust the health care systems due to past discriminatory experiences

☐ I have a fear of being discriminated against within the mental health community in the United States

☐ I lack health benefits

☐ My income is relatively low-wage

☐ I have language barriers

- ☐ Pressures of work keep me from practicing mental health hygiene or self-care
- ☐ My legal status prevents me from engaging in mental health hygiene
- ☐ I have a challenge identifying practitioners who are not only competent but are able to provide bilingual or monolingual Spanish-speaking services
- ☐ Cultural differences can affect the care I get from mental health providers
- ☐ Many practitioners are not aware of my idioms and expressions used to describe stress and mental distress
- ☐ There is a lack of information about where to seek mental health services
- ☐ There is a lack of information in Spanish
- ☐ There is a lack of the availability of tools that can be easily integrated into my culture and lifestyle

Now that you have been able to identify some barriers or stigmas, I want you to take the time to understand, challenge, and investigate each of these checked stigmas. Here is a suggestion on how to start:

- Learn more about mental health
- Allow yourself to have a beginner's mind attitude
- Bring a sense of curiosity instead of fear towards mental health hygiene

Self-Generated Mental Health Stigmas

Self-generated fear, barriers, and stigmas are strongly connected to family and community generated factors; however, these internal factors are basically the feeling of being responsible or guilty of the distress happening. Again, take some time to identify which of these statements are true for you.

CHECK THE ONES THAT APPLY[5]:

- ☐ All people with mental illness are dangerous; they will not recover, and their mental illness is their own fault
- ☐ I am afraid of being isolated or rejected within my community because I engage in mental health care
- ☐ I feel guilty about being depressed or being diagnosed with a mental health illness
- ☐ I must act like everything it's ok even if it's not the case
- ☐ I should be able to cope with mental health problems myself
- ☐ My lack of knowledge causes fear and/or anxiety about mental illness
- ☐ Mental health treatment and the use of antidepressants can create ideas about being 'crazy'
- ☐ The use of antidepressants is associated with illegal drug use
- ☐ I have significant concerns about the strength and the addictive potential of mental health medications

Mental health illnesses are curable, like the flu, or a more serious bodily illness, like cancer. The biggest generator of fear behind the word 'mental health' is that it highlights a field of the unknown, right? In the Latinx culture, we use idioms such as *locura* (madness) as a representation of inexplicable behavior, and that term carries strong negative connotations. Someone who is *loco* (crazy) is seen as severely mentally ill, potentially violent and incurable[6]. As a community, we tend to label a family member with mental illness as suffering from *nervios* (nerves) which serves to destigmatize that person's experience both in the family and the community. This is true for my family and for me; is it for you? If it's not, congratulations! You and your family may be well informed around mental health and proper use of idioms.

There is a better way to live and manage the stress we all face as humans on a daily basis, and more as immigrants of a new culture, language, and country. It is important to understand that mental health hygiene means that we care about being in balance internally and externally.

REFLECTIVE QUESTIONS:

- What are some mental health stigmas you identified that you are willing to work with?

    o Yourself

_____

_____

_____

    o your family

_____

_____

_____

    o your culture

_____

_____

_____

- What are some mental health stigmas that are keeping you from practicing mental health hygiene?

    o Self-generated

    _____

    _____

    _____

    o Family-Community generated

    _____

    _____

    _____

- How can you lower your fear towards mental health hygiene, care, and illnesses?

    _____

    _____

    _____

- After learning a little about mental health stigmas, what steps can you take towards learning more about mental health hygiene?

    _____

    _____

    _____

Identify Mental Habits and Patterns

"Life isn't as serious as my mind makes it out to be"

Eckhart Tolle[1]

The main stress trigger is our perception of things and of the world.[2] Perception could be explained as the way we see and take what we see, sense, hear, and experience. Are you aware of the voice in your head? That voice that gives you an opinion on all you do that tells you to go or not go to the gym, that comments on the people who walk by and sit next to you – yes, that voice talking to you now! This voice is unique in each of us, and at times it brings negative patterns and habits that have been cultivated by past experiences and exposures. The biggest step you can take in this process is to acknowledge this voice of perception and know that thinking without awareness of our thoughts is the biggest dilemma of our human existence[3]. Mindfulness starts the minute we become aware or notice that we are thinking, creating opinions or planning things, etc.

Why is perception important? Because the attention we give to observe and learn about our positive, negative or neutral mental habits can allow us to identify stressors that cause us pain and suffering.

What is a Stressor?

The most crucial thing that you can do to work with stress is to learn to identify when it starts to happen. These patterns are usually awakened by something that happened in the past, and when these triggers are touched, they cause pain in us[1]. So how do we start identifying them? Look out for these signs:

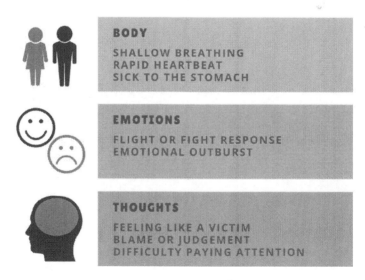

BODY
SHALLOW BREATHING
RAPID HEARTBEAT
SICK TO THE STOMACH

EMOTIONS
FLIGHT OR FIGHT RESPONSE
EMOTIONAL OUTBURST

THOUGHTS
FEELING LIKE A VICTIM
BLAME OR JUDGEMENT
DIFFICULTY PAYING ATTENTION

Source: See Notes[1]

The greatest gift I have given myself was the knowledge to understand and dedicate the time to learn about my internal world. Once you start pausing and taking the time to reflect on why any of these signs are happening, you will begin to learn what your stress triggers are. Take some time to learn how to work with triggers by doing mindfulness practice #2.

Self-regulation

Once you know what your triggers are, you can start self-regulating. What do I mean by that? You can notice and see what your stressors are, and start understanding and naming that feeling, thought or sensation. In self-regulation, we start to move from compulsive behaviors into choices[1]. What do I mean? It means that you can pause, identify that emotion or thought is taking over you and make a choice to let whatever has risen to pass through you before you fall into habitual reactions. Meditation and stillness or sitting practice will help you develop this skill. Believe me – I know how hard it can be to break a pattern of negative thoughts or behaviors! This week's meditation is based on this practice.

SELF-REGULATION

IS NOT...

- Suppress emotions
- Avoid emotions
- Deny emotions
- Not having some emotions

IS...

- Understand what we are feeling
- Know what this emotion means
- Observe our preferences, tendencies and behaviors
- Become skillful with our emotions
- Know when each emotion is appropriate

Sources: See Notes[2]

REFLECTIVE QUESTIONS:

• What are some of words you use to express your mental distress?

_____

_____

_____

_____

• Describe your thoughts, physical sensations, and emotions that arise when you read your immigration story from week 2.

_____

_____

_____

_____

• What issues do I have in communicating and understanding the American culture?'

_____

_____

_____

_____

- Describe your journey learning English as a second language

_____

_____

_____

_____

_____

- How often have you stopped to reflect on your immigrations story and circumstances? How does it feel to pause and reflect?

_____

_____

_____

_____

_____

MINDFULNESS ACTIVITIES:

1. *Rompiendo* (Breaking) Stigmas!

☐ Choose a close friend or family member to have a candid conversation about mental health hygiene tools
☐ Ask about what techniques they do to care for their internal wellbeing
☐ Choose one practice and do it twice this week

☐ Share with a loved one about your experience (if <u>not</u> enrolled in a class)

☐ Share your thoughts about your experience with the online class (if enrolled in a class)

2. *El Trensito* (The train)[1]

This mindfulness exercise is used to work with triggers. There are five steps that you will take once you identify the stress trigger in your body, emotions or thoughts.

3.   Mental Health Stigmas Online Test

☐ Visit this page: https://www.curestigma.org
☐ It takes less than 5 minutes to complete
☐ Reflect on the results and questions being asked.

MEDITATION PRACTICE:

Connecting with stillness (Self-regulation Meditation)

• Length: 10 minutes
• Practice five (5) times this week

This meditation can help embrace uneasiness and any types of discomfort happening either in the emotionally, mentally or physically.

Optional: Practice twice (2) this week Self-Timed Silent Breathing Meditation (no audio).
For guided meditation, go to www.almayespiritu.com/guidedmeditations
Password to access: pertenæcer

Week 5

Getting to Know Emotions

Week 5 – Getting to Know Emotions

"El corazón alegre es buena medicina"
Translation: A heart that is happy is the best medicine.

Proverbio 17:22[1]

So, we already talked about the voice in our heads, known as our mind, or also defined as the subjective experience in week one. Do you recall? If not, I invite you to revisit week one. The reason I am mentioning the mind or this subjective experience is that our emotions are a complex process that involves our mind (subjective experience), our body (physiological response), and our actions (expressive response)[2]. Therefore, emotions are the main character in the development of stress[3]. This graphic will help you see the relationship among mind, body, and action while we experience an emotion[2].

Source: see notes[2]

What is an Emotion?

Our emotions, in essence, are impulses to act[1]. Last week, we learned about Self-regulation; this week we learn about these emotions we are trying to regulate and understand because our goal is to befriend all our emotions[2]. When we are not monitoring or understanding our emotions, they take over and control our lives, and at times they sabotage our abilities to succeed at work and have a clear mind[3].

When I was experiencing high levels of anxiety and stress, my mind was out of my control, so my thoughts triggered physical responses plus reactive emotional actions. Why was this happening? Because I had no idea about my negative mental patterns (thoughts) that led me into trains of thought that created stress. Once I was able to differentiate and pay attention to what was happening in my head and body, I was able to slowly stop myself from having negative emotional reactivity take over me. This is not an easy process; it takes time, and I still have to work with pausing and self-regulation to manage strong emotions. But before we continue talking about befriending emotions, I want to highlight that there are four basic universal emotions associated with stress: fear, anger, sadness, and happiness[4]. The first three most people consider negative emotions – but why? These are emotions essential for our survival. Fear, anger, and sadness do bring along sensations and thoughts that are not enjoyable but let's take some time to truly understand what these emotions are and how they manifest in our bodies[5].

Take a few minutes to reflect on this *Dicho* about emotions.

"No le eches leña al fuego"

Translation: Do not add fuel to the fire. [a]

Understanding Fear

fear

The main function of fear is to identify a threat; this threat automatically activates the sensation of wanting to evade or run away. When fear is presented in our mind, immediately our thoughts evolve around fear[1]. This emotion is originated in humans because of the historical need to survive against predators. Nowadays it helps us plan, prepare, defend, and protect ourselves and our loved ones, and allows us to avoid danger. At times, fear can be excessive and cause secondary emotions such as anguish, tension, burdens, nervousness/edginess, insecurity, distrust, apprehension, misgiving, wariness, dread, fright (*Angustia, tensión, agobio, nerviosismo, inseguridad, desconfianza, recelo, duda, cautela, aprensión, susto*)[2]. As it happened to me, fear became the ruler of my mind and thoughts, so eventually, this fear turned into anxiety. As explained by Andres Martin Asusero in the context of stress, fear transforms into anxiety, and if fear and anxiety are constant, they can turn into panic[2]. In the first week, I shared my experience with a panic and anxiety attack while I was riding in my sister's car; this week we are learning about the emotion that triggered this reaction in me. I do not want to cultivate fear in you; instead, I want to inform you of what happens when we do not take care of ourselves, our mental habits, and our minds. In this guidebook, we are learning mental hygiene through mindfulness and meditation practices – why? Because it is scientifically proven to help cope with stress[3], and because it worked for me.

Fear is also the main cause of unhealthy behaviors, such as impatience, rushing, perfectionism, submission, indecisiveness, fear of taking a risk, and obsessive-compulsive behaviors, as well as lying and betrayal[2].

As immigrants, we also face fear in many forms; some ways our fear of being vulnerable, fear of getting hurt, fear of the pain of disconnection, fear of criticism, fear of failure, or fear of not measuring up[4]. The pain we face as immigrants when being discriminated against or isolated can turn either into fear or hate[5]. It doesn't have to be this way; we turn to fear and pain into love and compassion[6]. This is not an easy process, but it is doable if you are willing to take a chance! Next week we will learn about compassion and how to cultivate it, so sit tight!

Understanding Anger

Anger is another emotion tightly tied to fear and stress; however, instead of wanting to run away, we get the urge to fight against the threat. At times anger can help us in practicing healthy competition and fight against injustices and rights, and can act as a defense mechanism against circumstances that we cannot run away from that can help in our survival. In other instances, anger can awaken other emotions like tension, annoyance, aggressiveness, frustration, fury, resentment, indignation, animosity, annoyance, irritability, and hostility (*Tensión, molestia, agresividad, frustración, furia, resentimiento, indignación, animosidad, molestia/fastidio, irritabilidad, enemistad)*[1, 2]. Untreated anger can manifest in violence, cardiovascular disorders, and depression. Anger also brings a lot of feelings of shame and isolation to those who are not able to be in control of it[1].

Suppressing anger slowly takes away our joy and spirit, and when we express it, it takes away our ability to make changes and connect. Like fear, anger can also be transformed, transformed into courage, love, change, compassion, and justice. If anger is hiding another emotion, such as grief, regret, or shame, we can instead use that emotion to investigate what is happening within us. If we don't take the time to transform this emotion, it will turn into bitterness and resentment[2]. As I mentioned in the fear section, compassion will be a focus in week six. And in week seven, we will learn how to work with shame as an antidote to anger. Just keep in mind, we are transforming our subjective experience so we can embrace all emotions, and drive our actions from a place of understanding, love, and care.

Understanding Sadness

Sadness appears when we cannot run away with fear or fight with anger. Instead, it connects us with reflection and introspective. It allows us to learn from our mistakes, to ask for help, and to heal losses in life[1]. This emotion connects us with the need to care for ourselves and receive care from others while we reflect and elaborate on what is happening. In some cases, too much sadness leads to apathy, disappointment (*apatía, desinterés/desilusión*), or, if sadness is chronic, it turns into depression. A potential cause for depression is about a discrepancy in our behavior and deep personal values; therefore, depression can be an opportunity to bring balance in life's objectives and personal values[1].

Secondary emotions that emerge from sadness are grief, sorrow, cheerlessness, gloom, melancholy, self-pity, loneliness, dejection, and despair (*tristeza, tristeza, tristeza, tristeza, melancolía, autocompasión, soledad, abatimiento, desesperación*)[2].

In the process of trying to heal myself, I have been working on bringing this balance (actions and values) into my life at all levels, personally and professionally. It has not been easy, as our lives are very complex. The important thing here is to make the decision to dedicate the time to work on yourself, your wellbeing, and what is important for you. Leaving our home countries and comfort zones is not an easy decision; however, whatever emotion is present at this time, pause and think, "Is this trying to teach me or show me something?" Allow this room for reflection to help you transform your sadness into joy and wisdom.

Understanding Joy

The last of the four emotions is the one we love to experience, right? Joy gives ground to happiness, which is that sensation of fullness and presence, and connection with life as it is, without the need to change anything. In other words, it is complete satisfaction with things how they are. Joy allows us to connect with others, motivate, discover, and love. It is the basic emotion in love. On the other side, if we force joy in our lives, we can direct ourselves to live a life fantasizing about the future with unrealizable expectations; at times we try to find joy by consuming substances that generate this feeling in us. Forcing or creating artificial joy in our lives can create a lack of planning, the inability to deal with our problems, and the lack of reflection about life losses. It can also cause insensibility towards the pain and suffering of others, as well as a sense of arrogance[1].

A good example of this can be the image some people create on social media, where they only focus on portraying the presence of joy. As we have learned, joy is transitory, like any emotion; all other emotions are left out. This image can cause a sense of arrogance in others and personally can create stress and pressure to maintain and live up to this forced image of ultimate happiness and joy. Take some time this week to practice the second mindfulness practice focused on mindful social media sharing and interactions.

Mindfulness of Emotions

In week three, we learned about mindfulness. This week we will apply this behavior to our emotions. Here is a refresher – we will pay non-judgmental attention to the present moment without the need to react and with a sense of welcoming and openness to whatever emotion is present[1]. There is no need to suppress or reject what is happening in our bodies and minds; instead, we are seeing, listening, sensing, and trying to understand what is passing through us.

FEAR

Shaking, agitation, palpitations, back, neck, and shoulder tension, cold sweat, rapid breathing, knot in stomach. Blood circulates to our legs, our face gets pale because the blood is flowing to our legs. the body can also freeze waiting if the best reaction is to hide or run away.

ANGER

Same as the symptoms of a fear plus blood flow to the face, hands, and arms, heart rate increases, and adrenaline is generated to give us the energy to act.

HOW DO THESE EMOTIONS MANIFEST IN OUR BODY

SADNESS

Energy saving mode, tightness in chest, tension in throat, low or drop in energy, loss of enthusiasm in life's activities. slow metabolism.

JOY

Feeling of relaxation, expansion of chest, a smile arises, face relaxes, the desire for physical contact (hugs, laughs, singing, playing, jumping), increased energy, quieting of worrisome thoughts, a general sense of rest, readiness, enthusiasm.

Sources: see notes [2, 3]

REFLECTIVE QUESTIONS:

- What emotion/emotions has/have visited you while reading this section?

- How did this/these emotion/emotions manifest in your thoughts? Your body? And actions?

_____

_____

_____

_____

_____

- Is your subjective voice highly driven by fear, anger, sadness or joy?

_____

_____

_____

_____

_____

- What are some thought patterns you have been able to identify?

_____

_____

_____

_____

_____

- When is this emotion most prevalent? List a few scenarios, experiences or circumstances.

_____

_____

_____

_____

_____

- Which primary emotion prevails in your thought patterns?

_____

_____

_____

_____

- How does this emotion manifest in your body?

_____

_____

_____

_____

- Write down a few thought patterns you can identify while in this emotion.

_____

_____

_____

_____

_____

- Are your actions and behaviors aligned with your values?
  - If not, what steps can you take to align them?

_____

_____

_____

_____

- What secondary emotions can you identify and relate to the most in your everyday life?

_____

_____

_____

_____

- Write down a few thought patterns you can identify with this secondary emotion.

_____

_____

_____

_____

_____

MINDFULNESS ACTIVITIES:

1. What Am I Feeling Now?

- ☐ Choose 4 memories that generate these four basic emotions: FEAR, ANGER, SADNESS, and JOY
- ☐ Find a quiet space to sit and reflect without interruption
- ☐ Start with the easiest one for you (Try to choose manageable scenarios)
    - ☐ Recall the experience
    - ☐ Start writing what you are thinking aside from memory, describe your physical response to the physical experience and thoughts
    - ☐ Take some time to self-soothe by giving yourself a hug and practice this week's guided meditation

2. Mindful Social Media

This week I want you to take a pause before posting or commenting on social media. This is how you will practice:

- Start by choosing one social media platform
- Time yourself on time spent scrolling and navigating (Set a timer for 10 minutes)
- Once time is up – take a break
- Before posting or commenting take a deep breath and ask yourself:
  - What is my intention for this post and comment?
  - How do you want the person reading this to feel?
  - Will this comment or post affect anyone's state of mind or happiness?
- Once you have answered these questions go ahead and complete your post or comment
- Continue taking breaks and set healthy scrolling and navigating limits for yourself

MEDITATION PRACTICE:

Everything It's Ok, I'm Ok (Self-Compassion Meditation)

- Length: 10 minutes
- Practice five (5) times this week

This meditation is designed to help you cope with strong, negative, and disruptive emotions. It is the base of self-love and self-care practices.

Optional: Practice twice (2) this week Self-Timed Silent Breathing Meditation (no audio).
For guided meditation, go to www.almayespiritu.com/guidedmeditations
Password to access: pertenæcer

Week 6

Belonging in Me, My Family, and My Community

Week 6 – Belonging in Me, My Family, and My Community

Sometimes fear, anger, or sadness can be a wake-up call into the start of our personal transformation journey, as it happened to me. Some of us may reach a point in life where we may question our purpose; we may have been living a life full of agitation or anxiety, become numb to life, allowed pain, distress, anguish, fear, or hatred to take over our lives, or perhaps we may have faced traumatic experiences, or maybe we just want to work on ourselves. If these occurrences are true for you, it may seem confusing to confront so much pain and so many obstacles in our quest for happiness; our lives may seem instead full of suffering, unwanted change, and turmoil. It doesn't have to be this way. So how do we deal with this pain in a healthy way? As mentioned in the last chapter, unwelcoming emotions can be healed through compassion.

Dicho reflection: How does it relate to the concept of belonging?

"El sol sale para todos"
Translation: The sun shines for all. [a]

What is Compassion?

Compassion can be defined as the process of working through the resistance of our pain and suffering; in other words, we listen and sit with the physical and subjective experience that happens with our pain, and in this space, we start to actually feel the pain. We allow ourselves to experience compassion for ourselves, for others who are vulnerable, and for those who become unbalanced by their pain and therefore are lost in suffering[1]. With compassion for ourselves, we learn to respond to the suffering and pain with presence, acceptance, and an effort to try to understand the unknown.

Another way to apply compassion in our lives is by liberating ourselves, other people, and the world from the views that imprison them[2]. We see our suffering and others' pain as part of life, without the need to justify or judge – put others in a 'box.' Living without compassion separates us from others and limits us from engaging in a life that allows seeing the unrestricted, limitless, and boundless connection we have with ourselves, our families, and our communities.

Compassion in Spirituality and Religion

"Si rezar es hablar con Dios, meditar es escucharlo"
Translation: If prayer is a talk with God, then meditation is listening to him.
Davidji[1]

I think it is important to address the role of religion over our mental health hygiene and wellbeing. I want to clarify that this guidebook and any of the practices are not tied to any religious affiliation. So, what do I mean by this? As you may know already, religious practices focus on church attendance, reading scriptures, purification through religious actions, and the act of seeking emotional support and advice from clergy.

On the other hand, spiritual practices involve a broader concept where we explore our internal world and subjective experience and overall consciousness; in spirituality, there is no connection with any religious beliefs, doctrines, or denominations[2]. Why am I talking about this? Because many Latinxs, including myself, have a hard time separating the two. At times, we put religion and spirituality in the same category. When someone asks us about our faith, we at times answer, "I am a spiritual person, not religious." This can be true to an extent; however, being religious doesn't mean that we cannot explore our subjective experience and internal self, and vice versa, being spiritual doesn't mean we cannot attend or be part of the religious affiliation. The two can work harmoniously with each other; the medical field has already embraced mindfulness as a way to transform a person's attitude towards their illness[3]– see <u>Appendix B</u>. This entire guidebook is a tool to use in caring and working for our mental health hygiene. Therefore, the practices and concepts presented in this guidebook do extend into the spiritual quest of exploring our inner world.

Compassion arrives as a tool to help us cope with the emotions, thoughts, and physical discomforts that arise in the process of working with our subjective experiences. Mindfulness and meditation can be considered alternative healing practices.

According to research, the Latinx culture carries with it a sense of loss of control and ownership of our mental health and wellbeing, because at times we link faith and supernatural forces to what is happening inside of us in our subjective experience. I'm not saying this is true for all Latinxs, but just keep an open mind and if perhaps this is somewhat true for you, take this moment to allow yourself to learn a new perspective on this[4]. The new perspective eliminates the need to blame others or faith on what is happening to us, and instead, we take charge of our mental health by practicing the tools provided in this guidebook and deciding for ourselves if these tools are useful for our wellbeing.

Cultivating Compassion

"Bring forth song and celebration, so that the spirit will be alive among
us."

César Chávez[1]

Compassion practice is a mindfulness practice because when we
practice compassion, we become aware of the mental, emotional, and
physical sensations that are happening in us. But instead of just being the
observer of these states, we dedicate the time to comfort and offer kind
thoughts and feelings. We embrace with loving-kindness (genuinely

caring, understanding, and providing non-judgmental support) to whatever state is present in the body, mind, and heart[2].

When we transform our perspective from judging and being harsh on ourselves or others, and instead by deeply caring, understanding, and providing non-judgmental support, we start to view our problems from a different perspective, and no longer through the eyes of fear and obstructed reality. In this space, we begin to see the possibilities in good or bad situations, encountering the possibility of freedom, resolution, acceptance, creativity, compassion, and wisdom, which may have seemed almost inconceivable before[3]. Compassion does not mean to feel pity for yourself or others, it is instead the capacity to turn towards the pain and have the desire or act toward the relieving the suffering in ourselves and others[4].

In Self-Compassion, we[5]:

- Soothe and comfort ourselves
- Recognize that suffering (pain) is part of the human condition
- Validate our pain
- Accept the pain mindfully (without judgment or pity)
- Hold the pain with a loving presence so it can transform into love
  - o In Compassion with others, we[5]:
- Soothe and comfort (if possible)
  - o If not, send silent soothing and comforting thoughts and feelings
- Recognize that suffering (pain) is part of the human condition
- Validate the pain
- Accept the pain mindfully (without judgment or pity)

- Hold the pain with a loving presence so it can transform into love

These are not easy practices – I know! But I also know that meditation and mindfulness have allowed me to see the pain in me and in others, and therefore I feel alive and connected, and not alone. Compassion meditation has taught me how to care and connect with others in many ways other than race, culture, language, or ethnicity. Through the practice of self-compassion and compassion with others, I guarantee that you will connect with feelings of belonging within yourself, your family, and your communities. This week's meditation will plant the seed for your journey into compassion.

Why practice compassion? Personally, it is one of my favorite practices. I have learned to soothe and care for myself, and for others in a healthy and not-draining way. It is also because the studies visited for the development of this curriculum recommend that Compassion practices should be emphasized in Latinx populations[6]. As you may have already sensed in yourself, we (Latinxs) tend to be highly compassionate people. As a collectivist culture, we care for the well-being of the group, but keep-in-mind that at times we may forget about our personal needs.

REFLECTIVE QUESTIONS:

- Based on what you have learned, how do you compare prayer to meditation?

_____

_____

_____

_____

- What other mental hygiene practices have you heard of? Choose one that you are familiar with. How does it compare to meditation?

_____

_____

_____

_____

- How do you define compassion? Share a recent experience where you felt compassion for another person.

_____

_____

_____

_____

- From your personal experience do you think compassion is different than empathy? (In week seven we will review empathy, for now, base it on your own definition)

_____

_____

_____

_____

- Describe one or two recent scenarios where compassion was present in you. How did it feel mentally, emotionally, and physically?

_____

_____

_____

_____

- What thoughts are present when compassion is present in you?

_____

_____

_____

_____

MINDFULNESS ACTIVITIES:

1. Cooking with Family!

- ☐ Reach out to a friend or family member and request a recipe (Ideally from your native culture)
- ☐ Ask for guidance on how to make the recipe
- ☐ Prepare the meal in silence without company (no music or distractions) or with others (no music or conversation, only communication about tasks)
- ☐ Enjoy the meal in silence with or without company
- ☐ At the end of the meal you may express gratitude and/or share with company or online group about being in silence while cooking (if alone and not in an online class, write thoughts on your journal or call a friend/relative to share)

2. A Celebration of Diversity Through Music

- Think of a song that reminds you of connection and celebration from your native country
  - ○ Here are some ideas:
    - ▪ José Luis Rodríguez - Agárrense de las Manos (Venezuela)
    - ▪ Jorge Negrete - México Lindo (México)
    - ▪ Jorge Paladino - La Cumbia Chinandegana (Nicaragua)
    - ▪ Guantanamera - Celia Cruz (Cuba)
    - ▪ Tita Merelo - Se Dice de Mi (Argentina)
    - ▪ Lalo Rodriguez - Devorame Otra Vez(Puerto Rico)
    - ▪ Aniceto Molina - El Campanero (Colombia)
- Find lyrics to the song

- Play and sing along with the song
- Optional – play again and dance with family or friends this song
- If enrolled in an online group, share the song and lyrics with the instructor by suggested deadline

MEDITATION PRACTICE:

Connecting with Compassion through Loving-kindness (Compassion Meditation)

- Length: 20 minutes
- Practice five (5) times this week

This week's meditation will help you establish a deep sense of positive interconnectedness (see week seven) to others, regardless of where you think you belong[1].

Optional: Practice twice (2) this week Self-Timed Silent Breathing Meditation (no audio).

For guided meditation, go to www.almayespiritu.com/guidedmeditations
Password to access: pertenæcer

Week 7

We are One World

Week 7 – We are One World

One of the *dichos* (sayings) included in at the beginning of this guidebook was *"Mi casa es tu casa"* (My home is your home). In just a few words, this *Dicho* wraps around what it means to be a Latinx. Our diverse cultures have in common what is called *Personalismo* (Personification) which emphasizes the importance of having smooth interpersonal relationships through warm, friendly, and personal interactions[1]. How do we embody *personalismo*? According to research, Latinxs use *Personalismo* to define their self-worth by taking into consideration the inner qualities that give them self-respect, an inner sense of dignity, and the ability to earn the respect of others[2]. This is just research…is it true for you? Take some time to reflect in your journal and answer the questions from the reflective section at the end of this week.

This concept of *Personalismo* may or may not be true for you. However, human beings and everything on this planet are interconnected in some way. Why is this approach important? Because in this process of belonging to ourselves, our families, our communities, and the world we must welcome the perspective that we are all interconnected.

What is Interconnectedness?

It means that we are all in this together[1], that we are all connected in some way to one another, no matter our language, race, culture, or anything else. Interconnectedness brings along a new perspective that can help us in working with our feelings of isolation and not belonging. As research has shown, people with the ability to weave, relate and create relationships within both cultures (American and your native one) have a sense of interconnectedness, and this becomes an important component of not only acquiring cultural content but establishing social support networks[4]. Also, this ability to engage in a balanced way both cultures can be a mechanism that protects Latinxs from increased psychological problems[2]

Interconnectedness

Understanding Empathy

It is interesting to note that empathy in our brain was discovered by someone who accidentally picked up food in front of a monkey![1] The researchers found that humans and monkeys have what is called "Mirror neurons," these neurons allow us to mimic what others do and vice versa; therefore, they are the neural basis of empathy[1]. Empathy is born form self-awareness; this means that the more in-tune we are with our own emotions, the more skilled we become in reading others' feelings. It is that ability to know how the other feels[2].

Take a break - How would you connect this traditional *Dicho* to the concept of empathy?

> # "¡Ponte en mis zapatos!"
> Translation: Put yourself in my shoes. [a]

Cultivating Empathy

It is important to say that at the beginning of my journey into learning about myself and my subjective experience, I didn't know the difference between empathy and compassion. In a way, I thought that compassion was more like pity, but as we have learned, compassion has to do with the desire to free yourself and others of pain and suffering, a sense of alleviation. On the other hand, empathy comes into play as the emotion that allows us to sense and be in the place of the other. How can we do this? By learning about how it feels (mentally, physically, and emotionally) to be angry, sad, annoyed, nervous, etc. As we pay attention to our non-verbal channels, like our own tone of voice, gestures, and facial expressions, we are learning how to tune to others' reactions[1].

In training our mind and ourselves to be more empathetic, we switch our thought pattern from the action, and more into the distress/reaction caused on others by our behavior/actions. We empathize consequences and self-awareness of what we may feel if we were on the other side. This is not an easy process when we are feeling drained and unable to cope with our own stress and worries. It took me a long time before I could put myself in the shoes of others, it took a lot of self-compassion and understanding that the pain of others doesn't need to be taken; instead, it can be transformed. How do we transform it? Through mindful compassion practices, and lovingkindness (see the mindfulness and meditations from week 6, 7, 8).

Empathy and compassion will arm us with love-based tools to cope with the pain caused by discrimination and ignorance we face as immigrants in the United States. We cannot change the other; however, we can change the way we hear and take on what others say. In this graphic, you will see how we can react with empathy and/or compassion when facing discrimination. Take time to practice the Just Like Me Meditation; it will help you oversee and overcome the differences and find the similarities between those that you may like or not like so much.

Scenario: We are in a store speaking Spanish with a family member, and someone approaches us and says, "Speak English; go back to your country." How could we react with either empathetic or compassionate thought patterns?

- Take a deep-breath and rationalize empathetically:

  o What would make me react this way towards another person speaking a language that is not the dominant one in the country I live?
  o How would it feel if people moved to my home country legally/illegally and spoke their native tongue around the country?
  o How would it feel to not understand what other people are saying?
  o How would it feel to not know other cultures?
  o How would it feel to be exposed to people that don't fit the stereotype within our comfort zone?

- Take a deep-breath and rationalize compassionately:

  - I may not know why this person is doing this, but something inside of them causes anger towards this situation
  - Whatever is happening inside this person, is not personal, and doesn't mean that everyone feels this way
  - I hope this person can overcome this fear/anger/resentment that he/she/they may be feeling
  - I don't know the circumstances that may have led this person to react this way; however, I understand that they are acting from a place that they think is the best for them

- If possible, try to engage with this person in a rational, safe discussion
  - What would you like to know about my choice to speak Spanish?
  - What would you want to know about my decision to leave my home-country?

- If it's not, do not respond, and distance yourself from the incident

- Allow time to practice self-compassion and soothing for the pain that may have been caused by this incident.

REFLECTIVE QUESTIONS:

- How do you measure your self-worth?

- How does the opinion of others about you affect your self-worth?

- Do you relate to the *personalismo* concept? If so, how?

- What inner qualities provide you with a sense of self-respect?

  _____

  _____

  _____

  _____

  _____

- What inner qualities provide you with an inner sense of dignity?

  _____

  _____

  _____

  _____

  _____

- What inner qualities provide you with the ability to earn the respect of others?

  _____

  _____

  _____

  _____

  _____

- Has your definition of empathy changed from chapter six?

- What is a recent experience that made you feel empathy?

- Describe a recent experience where you decided to send compassion to another instead of empathy.

- Mention 2-3 incidents where you think compassion will be better than empathy.

_____

_____

_____

_____

_____

- Mention 2-3 scenarios where empathy should be present instead of compassion.

_____

_____

_____

_____

_____

- Do you think we should be cautious with empathy? If so, why?

_____

_____

_____

_____

_____

Transforming Shame

Shame can become more present when we find ourselves as part of a minority and when we are faced with discriminatory situations in a new land. As Brené Brown explains, shame is that "intensely painful feeling or experience of believing that we are flawed and therefore unworthy of love and belonging – something we've experienced, done, or failed to do makes us unworthy of connection"[1]. This concept is a strong one and one that we as immigrants need to work with. I personally for many years felt shame for my culture, my skin color, my hair color, my accent, my family, my parents, and my language. Why do we develop shame as immigrants? Personally, I think it is because of discrimination and the urge to feel like we belong somewhere, even if its outside of who we are and where we come from. It has taken years for me to embrace and love who I am internally and externally, as well as who my family and my ancestors were and where they came from. I invite you to work with me in transforming these feelings of not being perfect or good enough into feelings of self-love and acceptance and thoughts that honor our culture, family, traditions, and history.

So how might that voice of shame sound for a Latinx? "I am different, and that's weird, I won't fit in," "People won't like you for who you are," "My traditions are aboriginal, people will make fun of me and my culture," "My parents don't speak English, it's embarrassing to talk about them," "My family didn't go to college, they don't understand the system, I'm afraid of others know this I will be rejected," "My accent makes me different, and exposed to discrimination," "I'm not pretty, my hair is dark, my eyes too, and I don't look like anyone in the movies or television," "I'm not worthy of asking for a race, I may get fired if I speak up," "I am not good enough for this job or career," etc... Do you identify with any of these? I do; my subjective experience and internal dialogue revolved around things like this when I was outside my comfort zone. Through loving-kindness and self-compassion meditation, plus lots of mindfulness of thought practice, I am able to monitor the voice of shame and replace it with the voice of self-love and acceptance and the voice that honors who I am and where I can from. Getting to this chapter and reading along with me is already a huge step in this journey of *Pertenæcer* (belonging and being reborn). **Congratulations!**

REFLECTIVE QUESTIONS:

- What experiences in life have made you feel shame?

_____

_____

_____

_____

_____

- What thoughts arise when shame is present in you?

_____

_____

_____

_____

_____

- How can you do to honor your ancestry with pride instead of shame?

- What can you learn about your past that you already don't know? What can help you connect with healthy pride of your ancestry, heritage, and culture?

MINDFULNESS ACTIVITIES:

1. Connecting over traditions that matter

- ☐ Write about your favorite holiday from your native country
  - ○ Which one is it?
  - ○ When is it celebrated?
  - ○ Why do you enjoy it?

- ☐ Pick a holiday you are unfamiliar with from the dominant culture in the US
  - o Learn about it
    - ▪ What is the holiday you picked?
    - ▪ When is it celebrated?
    - ▪ Why is it celebrated? Is it celebrated in the entire United States?
    - ▪ Is there any food tied to this holiday?
    - ▪ What do people do to celebrate it?
- ☐ In your journal write a short paragraph explaining the new-learned holiday tradition
- ☐ Share your new findings with two family members and ask if they were familiar with this holiday
- ☐ Share both holiday details with class (if enrolled in an online class)

2. Gratitude unites
- ☐ Get a pen and a piece of paper
- ☐ Set a timer for five (5) minutes
- ☐ Start the timer
- ☐ Take three (3) deep breaths
- ☐ Write all the things you are grateful for in your personal life and professional life.

3. Interconnectedness in our Food
- ☐ Choose 3 meals to practice gratitude for the food
- ☐ Once the food is served (restaurant or at home)
- ☐ Take a deep breath and in reflect on who would you like to thank for the meal in front of you, these are some ideas of phrases:
  - o Thank you to all the people that put their time and efforts to make this meal possible

- o Thank you to my family for the work and efforts to make this meal possible
- o Thank you to the farmers for the work and efforts to make this meal possible
- o Thank you for the animals who gave their lives or a part of them to nurture my health
- o Thank you for the animals who gave their lives or a part of them to nurture my health

MEDITATION PRACTICE:

Just Like Me Meditation (Insight Meditation)[1]

- Length: 15 minutes
- Practice five (5) times this week

In this practice, the participant will experience a sense of identity with others. The idea is to create the potential to dissolve the sense of social distance or even enmity that may exist as part of our personal experiences as immigrants[1].

Optional: Practice twice (2) this week Self-Timed Silent Breathing Meditation (no audio).
For guided meditation, go to www.almayespiritu.com/guidedmeditations
Password to access: pertenæcer

Week 8

Belonging in Life Mindfully

Week 8 – Belonging in Life Mindfully

"Después de la tormenta viene la calma"
Translation: After the storm, calmness arrives.[a]

I want to close this guide by reflecting together with this last *Dicho*. What does this mean to you about all that we have learned? For me, it means that to have hope and optimism. What does it mean for you?

After completing this guidebook, I invite you to welcome optimism, and hope[1], as the main attitudes and states of minds in your everyday life. We (Latinxs immigrants) are well aware that we do not fit in the norm in the United States, we now know that we do not have to fit in, instead, we can carry our uniqueness, and be ourselves. Our stories, our accents, our cultures, our heritage, our traditions, our values, and our races are what makes us unique and who we are. Being aware of our uniqueness is a positive thing, and it is the biggest step in our self-love journey. Truly knowing ourselves allows us to embrace our roots and our ancestry, in a way that we carry an invisible (but perceptible) and amicable-pride.

What is Hope?

Hope gives the opportunity to wait for the storm to pass (as we saw in this weeks' *dicho*). As explained by psychologist C.R Snyder, Hope is "believing you have both the will and the way to accomplish your goals, whatever they may be."[1] People with high hope set higher goals, can self-motivate, find ways to accomplish things, are flexible with goals, and can make things more manageable by breaking things down or sorting them out[1].

Personally, there was a point in my life that I got lost in the day-to-day (rushing to work and rushing through life); silently I had lost hope, being a news broadcaster in this new country was not becoming a reality. I felt lost and allowed life to drive me around life. Anxiety attacks brought me back to life, they allowed me to slow down and reflect on life - reflect on what I was doing with my life and what was important for me in life. In the two years that I worked alone in my own self-healing, I came to understand that there was a better way to live and that I was eager to find it, learn it, and apply it so I could share it with the world. News broadcasting was no longer the only dream I had. I discovered that behind that dream I intended to be the voice of others and to help people. I'm not perfect or enlightened or a superior being, I'm just a regular Latinx immigrant that learned and continues to learn about how to live a better life in a world where we all feel like we don't belong. I have HOPE that this guidebook can help you, and many others feel connected to me and to all the other immigrants suffering and struggling in everyday life. Take time to reflect on hope in your life.

REFLECTIVE QUESTIONS:

- What keeps you pushing forward in life?

- What are some personal goals that give you hope in life?

- What are some professional goals that give you hope in life?

- Are your personal goals manageable? If no, how can you break them up or adjust them?

- Are your professional goals manageable? If no, how can you break them up or adjust them?

- List three things you are grateful for in your personal life

- List three things you are grateful for in your professional life

What is Optimism?

Daniel Goleman describes optimism as "having a strong expectation that, in general, things will turn out all right in life, despite setbacks and frustrations."[1] Psychologist Martin Seligman explains that optimism can be seen in people that see failure as something that can be changed and that will allow them to succeed the next time around. On the other side, pessimist blames themselves for the failure and see failure as something inevitable that they cannot change[2].

From my personal experience, I have had moments in life where I have been extremely optimistic, and others where I have been pessimistic. Being an immigrant and a minority in the United States means that we must work harder and longer to accomplish our goals and dreams. It is crucial that optimism is the main driver of our thoughts. Without optimism, we will not be able to achieve our American Dream- whatever it is for you. Do not let your accent, discrimination, others' ignorance, or your own fears stop you from getting where you want to get. In this journey of belonging you must become your best ally, friend, and supporter.

The Power of Mindfulness and Meditation in Everyday Life

In chapter three I listed the benefits of mindfulness and meditation, here is a list of how I have cultivated these benefits and continue to cultivate them every day in my life. The purpose of these practices is to help us feel like we belong to ourselves, our families, our communities, and our world.

HOW TO	BENEFITS	TOOLS FROM THIS GUIDEBOOK

BELONG IN ME	• Better pain tolerance
	• Emotional Regulation
	• Less stress-related body aches
	• Discovering new ways to cope more effectively with existing conditions difficulties, pain or suffering
	• Build your ability to focus
	• Increase self-knowledge and self-love
	• Learning to take better care of oneself
		• Self-regulation Meditation
		• Breathing Meditation (5-20 minutes)
		• Mindfulness of Body Meditation (10-20 minutes)
		• Doing Mindfulness Practices like the ones in this guidebook:
		  o My Breath is My Home
		  o Connecting with My Body
		  o Mindful Cleansing
		  o El Trensito (The Train)
		  o What Am I Feeling Now?
		  o Mindful Social Media

BELONG IN MY FAMILY	• More compassion and empathy
	• Build a good relationship with change
	• Regain the lost energy of trying to control everything
		• Breathing Meditation (5-20 minutes)
		• Compassion and Self-Compassion Meditation (5-20 minutes)
		• Doing Mindfulness Practices like the ones in this guidebook:
		  o Mindful Connection
		  o Ancestral Greeting
		  o A Celebration of Diversity Through Music
		  o Cooking with Family!

HOW TO	BENEFITS	TOOLS FROM THIS GUIDEBOOK

BELONG IN MY COMMUNITY	• Increased awareness and concentration
	• More efficiency in the things you do at home and at work
	• Fewer mistakes and conflict at home and at work
		• Breathing Meditation (5-20 minutes)
		• Compassion and Self-Compassion Meditation (5-20 minutes)
		• Doing Mindfulness Practices like the ones in this guidebook:
		  o Rompiendo (Breaking) Stigmas!
		  o Gratitude Unites
		  o Connecting over Traditions that Matter

BELONG IN THE WORLD	• Learn to be more present and aware	• Breathing Meditation (5-20 minutes) • Compassion and Self-Compassion Meditation (5-20 minutes) • Doing Mindfulness Practices like the ones in this guidebook: o *Pertenæcer* in Nature (Belonging and being reborn in nature)

REFLECTIVE QUESTIONS:

- Look up the definition of positivism. How does it differ from optimism?

- What is your definition of failure?

- How can you use failure as fuel to reach your goals in life?

- Do you consider yourself a positive or optimistic person? If both or none, how do you define your outlook in life?

_____

_____

_____

_____

_____

- Which mind states do you think is healthier for you? Positivistic, Optimistic or other? Why did you choose this mind state?

_____

_____

_____

_____

_____

- After completing most of this guidebook, have you redefined your American Dream? If yes, what is it now?

_____

_____

_____

_____

- Is there an ancestor that you admire? If so, who and why?

_____

_____

_____

_____

- What type of ancestor would you want to be? List the traits and how would you like to be remembered.

_____

_____

_____

_____

- What advice would you like to pass on to your children and grand-children?

_____

_____

_____

_____

- List your short-term and long-term goals that can lead you into passing on your advice and also becoming the ancestor you want to be.

Short-term goals

_____

_____

_____

_____

_____

Long-term goals

_____

_____

_____

_____

- How can you break up or manage your goals so they are more attainable and less intimidating?

_____

_____

_____

_____

MINDFULNESS ACTIVITY:

Pertenæcer in nature (Belonging and being reborn in nature)

- ☐ Choose a park in your current location
- ☐ Choose a date to spend at least 2 hours at this park
- ☐ Pack a small blanket and your journal
- ☐ Find a nice spot to set your blanket and write
- ☐ Practice a short breathing meditation (3-5 minutes)
- ☐ Spend the rest of the time connecting and reflecting on nature
  - o Reflect on nature's beauty
  - o Reflect on the stillness of plants
  - o Reflect on the transitions of the weathers in the sky
- ☐ Remember to use Mindful Journaling practices where your writing includes the description of thought patterns, sensations, and emotions.

MEDITATION PRACTICE:

Pertenæcer Meditation (Insight Meditation)

- • Length: 20 minutes
- • Practice five (5) times this week

This last meditation will help us cultivate thoughts and feelings on belonging. It is a reminder that we all want to be safe, happy, and healthy; and most importantly that we belong. We belong to ourselves, our families, our communities, and our world.

Optional: Practice twice (2) this week Self-Timed Silent Breathing Meditation (no audio).

For guided meditation, go to www.almayespiritu.com/guidedmeditations

Password to access: pertenæcer

Thank you for embarking on this journey with me and welcome to the *Pertenæcer* Family!

Appendix A – Stress-related Idioms in Latinx Community

- *Mal de ojo:* (The Evil Eye) social relations that may contain inherent dangers to the equilibrium of an individual.
- Susto/espanto: (Fright) akin to an acute stress reaction
- *Empacho:* (Indigestion) related to complex interplay of physiological and social factors.
- *Nervios:* (Nerves) general state of distress related to life's "trials and tribulations". Labeling a family member with mental illness as suffering from *nervios* serves to destigmatize that person's experience both in the family and the community.
- *Ataque de nervios:* (Nervous breakdown or attack) severe stress response similar to panic attack. A dramatic expression of deep sadness and distress among Caribbean Latinxs. Some *ataques* that occur at culturally appropriate times such as at a funeral are culturally normative ways of expressing deep sadness; other *ataques* may signal the presence of an anxiety or depression disorder.
- *Locura:* (Madness) carries strong negative connotations. Someone who is *loco* (Crazy) is seen as severely mentally ill, potentially violent and incurable.
- *Ponerse de su parte:* (Contributing one's part) This attitude reflects the feeling that one should be strong enough to cope with life's problems on their own and with the help of family and not need to depend on the mental health system.
- *Nudo en el estómago:* (knot in the stomach) Represents sensation of fear.
- *Celajes:* (Cloudscape) Spiritual and religious experiences of visions, of hearing one's name called (often by a recently deceased relative) and perceiving presences are relatively common and non-pathological

experiences for some Latinxs. *Celajes* sometimes gets misinterpreted by mental health professionals as signs of psychosis.

NOTE: Somatization of distress is at times misunderstood as either hypochondriasis or a lack of ability to express the psychological dimensions of emotional distress–neither of which is accurate. Rather Latinxs express depression and anxiety through a mix of physical and emotional complaints.

Idioms of Resilience

- *Si se puede* (yes, you can)
- *En la lucha* (in the struggle)
- *Echándole ganas* (making an effort)
- *En la unión esta la fuerza* (strength in numbers)
- *No hay mal que por bien no venga* (every cloud has a silver lining)
- *Querer es poder* (where there is a will, there is a way)

Sources: see notes [1,2,3]

Appendix B – Research-based Benefits from Mindfulness and Mindfulness Based Stress Reduction Programs

According to the University of Massachusetts page for Mindfulness Based Programs, MBSR is offered as a complement to traditional medical and psychological treatments, not as a replacement, and it is proven to be effective in helping to treat these conditions[1]:

- Panic Attacks
- Work related stress
- Family related stress
- Financial stress
- Asthma
- Cancer
- Chronic Illness
- Depression
- Eating Disturbances
- Fatigue
- Fibromyalgia
- Gastro-intestinal Distress
- Grief
- Headaches
- Heart Disease
- High-blood Pressure
- Pain
- Post-traumatic Stress
- Skin Disorders
- Sleep Problems

For more info see notes[1]

Other sources also list these conditions as treatable with mindfulness [2,3]:

- ADHD
- Anger
- Reduced Rumination
- Less emotional reactivity/more effective emotion regulation
- Increased focus
- More cognitive flexibility
- Improved working memory

For more info see notes [2,3]

Appendix C - Latinx Culturally-attuned Mental Health Services

- National Resource Center for Hispanic Mental Health
  http://www.nrchmh.org/
- Center for Latino/a Mental Health
  https://www.thechicagoschool.edu/center-for-research-and-practice-latino-mental-health/
- Latino Mental Health Providers Network
  https://lmhpn.tcscenters.org/
- The National Latino Behavioral Health Association (NLBHA)
  http://www.nlbha.org/
- Latino Behavioral Health Services
  http://latinobehavioral.org/
- National Alliance on Mental Health - Latino Mental Health
  https://www.nami.org/find-support/diverse-communities/latino-mental-health
- Latino Service Providers
  http://latinoserviceproviders.net/mental-health-resources/
- La Mesita Latino Mental Health Provider Network
  http://elfuturo-nc.org/language/en/professional-training/la-mesita-latino-mental-health-network/
- Latino Mental Health Program at Cambridge Health Alliance
  https://www.challiance.org/cha-services/specialty-services
- Latinx Therapy Online Directories (Find a local therapist)
  https://latinxtherapy.com/
  https://www.therapyforlatinx.com

Research behind PERTENÆCER

Introduction

As a Latin American, immigrant, mindfulness advocate, and mindfulness practitioner, I continue to see, both face-to-face and in research, low engagement rates in mental health care and hygiene in my community. With the existing and new waves of adult or late-immigrants coming to the United States, it was crucial to develop a culturally-attuned mindfulness guidebook that could help us cope with the acculturative stress encountered in the process. This guidebook's hope was to bring engagement in mental health hygiene by using the presented culturally adapted mindfulness and meditation practices as tools to cope with the acculturative stress of Latinxs in the United States.

Usage of Latinx through the Guidebook

Before jumping into the argument of how mindfulness was adapted and used as a mental health hygiene tool in the Latinx community, it is imperative for me to address why I use the term Latinx instead of Latino/a or Hispanic in this project. As explained in a recent article in Time magazine, the term Latinx was first used in college campuses "as a gender-neutral term that young people were using because they were 'tired of reaffirming the patriarchy inherent in language'"[1]. I intend to create a sense of welcoming and accepting language, and an environment where any person from Latin American origin no matter their race, gender, sexual orientation, religious belief, or cultural background feels safe and accepted. As stated in the same article, Latinx is a term that can be used "as the perfect label for a group that is hard to define"[1]. Even more, I use it as a sign of respect towards the diversity within this group. I am committed in my work to choose language and practices that have no limitations, that welcome diversity, and create a sense of interconnectedness and belonging.

A little bit of history, years before the emergence of this Latinx term, the most common terms used to refer to people from Latin America origins living in the United States were Latino or Hispanic. As Carteret[2] explains,

The term Latino denotes all persons living in the United States whose origins can be traced to the Spanish-speaking regions of Latin American, including the Caribbean, Mexico, Central American, and South America. The term Hispanic was created by the U.S. federal government in the early 1970s in an attempt to provide a common denominator to a large and highly diverse population with connection to the Spanish Language.[2]

The term Latinx brings along inclusive connotation and positive intention, something I felt was missing from prior terms assigned to Latin American immigrants in the US.

Defining the Audience within the Latinx Immigrant Community in the United States

Based on findings, and from my perspective and experience, this project focuses on serving bilingual college educated Latinx late-immigrants in the United States. The section concentrates on research findings that helped in choosing the audience.

Research shows that there is a need to address low rates of participation in mental health care from the Latinx community in the United States. One of the visited studies[1] focused on the role of therapy fears, ethnic identity, and spirituality on access to mental health care treatment among Latino college students. In this paper, various authors

160

come to agree that "[e]thnic minorities are at an increased risk. Research shows that ethnic minorities have a lower rate of utilization than Non-Hispanic Whites. Research indicates that correlates of psychotherapy use include help-seeking attitudes, mental health stigma, environmental constraints, affordability of services, and symptoms of distress"[1]. This research verifies that there is underutilization of mental health care in the Latinx community.

Additionally, in Falicov's[2] article on the wisdom and challenges of culturally attuned treatments for Latinxs, the author talks about specific needs within this group in the United States:

> [T]he growing population of Latino Immigrants and their children are the largest minority of potential consumers of mental health services in the next decades. The population included are primarily first-generation Spanish-speaking immigrants, with the largest number from Mexico, followed by Puerto Rico, and the smaller numbers from Central and South America.[2]

This research supports the need for mental health services and defines a specific audience within the Latinx group. Now, mental health care is not only about mindfulness and meditation; the mental health field is massive, and this project attempts to address a small portion of the need, by creating mental health hygiene tools for this group. The hope is that this training can help reshape negative help-seeking attitudes, demystify mental health stigmas, combat environmental constraints, open affordability of services, and ease the symptoms of distress.

In regards to engagement in mindfulness practices from this group, Olano, Kachan, Tannenbaum, Mehta, Annane, and Lee[3] researched the effect of sociodemographic factors on mindfulness practices in the US population. The study came to find that vulnerable population groups such as Latinos (the term used to refer to Latinx in this study) are less likely to engage in mindfulness practices and thereby less likely to benefit from potential health benefits; the researchers also advise the field of mindfulness interventions to prioritize serving minorities[3]. This study helped solidify the need for such practices in my community.

Guarnaccia, Martinez, and Acosta[4] studied the most prominent minorities within the Latinx community in the US: Mexicans, Puerto Ricans, and Cubans. In that study, the authors came to learn a great deal about the barriers Latinos face in accessing mental health care. These barriers exist at the individual, community, service system, and broader societal levels. What we know much less about is how to effectively overcome these barriers. The next generation of services research needs to test strategies for effectively bringing Latinos in need into mental health treatment.[4]

Once again, research demonstrates the need and the barriers that the field faces from this diverse group of people, such barriers have been taken into serious consideration in the development of this project.

It is important to clarify that not all research supports the need and the absence of participation from Latinxs. Bermúdez, Kirkpatrick, Hecker, and Torres-Robles[5] reviewed in their study the help-seeking attitudes of Latino families seeking family therapy, and they share that "Latinos do use formal counseling services and they have similar attitudes as non-Latinos about counseling, however, more research is needed to support these findings"[5]. These findings intrigued me and led me to continue to attempt identifying a group within the Latinx community that is in higher need of service.

Therefore, the research from Torres[6] touched on the intercultural competence traits that lead Latinxs to have success in the United States. He explained that

> [s]trong waves of immigration along with relatively high birthrates have resulted in large numbers of Latinos living in the United States. These individuals are faced with having to navigate the mainstream U.S. culture as well as their growing and changing ethno cultural enclaves. In order to successfully negotiate these different cultural contexts, individual must develop a set of skills that promotes effective adaptation.[6]

This research directed me towards looking at those experiencing cultural shock and acculturative stress, as shown in this research the ability to adapt has a positive effect on Latinxs' success in the United States. In my quest, I needed to find out more on how acculturated Latinxs and the less acculturated are coping and doing as immigrants in the United States.

Acculturation looks at the assimilation trajectories of the vast diversity of cultures within the Latinx population; it looks at socioeconomic integration, how their beliefs, values, and behaviors are socially transmitted and shared, essentially the conditions in which they live in the US[7]. Evermore, Torres[6] research on the Latinx definition of success states that "acculturation studies focus on what changes occur in an individual's life during cultural adaptation but overlook how these processes take place"[6]. He continues to expand on this idea and links this ability to acculturate to healthy mental health; "[t]he ability to engage in a balanced set of intercultural competencies may be a mechanism that buffers Latinos from increased psychological problems, particularly those from later generations"[6]. In the next sections, I dig into studying the conditions of acculturated Latinxs, and the less acculturated Latinxs.

Lastly, Silva, Paris, and Añez[8] developed a set of questions to help inform the mental health assessment process and implications for community-based providers[8]. The questions revolve around community and family support, acculturative stress, migration history, idioms of distress and resilience, native language and communication preferences, and country of origin[8]. These questions led me to develop a short questionnaire that can help readers identify if the guidebook, *Pertenæcer* (To belong, to be reborn), is right for them.

Acculturated Latinxs

Findings demonstrated that not everyone who is an immigrant faces acculturative stress. There is a small group of immigrants that has been able to benefit from the use of mental health care and self-care tools. The ability to acculturate shows a positive impact on engagement and acceptance of mental health practices and treatments; as Garcia[1] explains, acculturated Latinxs can "process of social change that is both unilateral and unidimensional"[1]. The author explains it as a multidimensional view of values and practices, and the identification of both heritage culture and the receiving culture as interrelated and simultaneously occurring. In my own words, these Latinxs have developed the ability to balance and mix both sides of their native culture and the new culture.

Studies also show that those Latinxs who speak English and who are open to smoothly integrating the new American culture have better engagement rates and knowledge about mental health care, interventions, and choices. As confirmed in Craft, Crone, DeLeon, and Ajayi's[2] research

"When examining what Latino populations understand about mental health, much research has focused on acculturation. Research suggests that greater acculturation is related to less stigma and more willingness to seek mental health treatment"[2].

Torres'[3]study talks about Latinxs definition of success and states that "[w]ithin the Latino intercultural competence model, Perseverance represents the determination to persist particularly when experiencing difficult barriers...It could be the case that it is the ability to persevere in the face of social injustice that allows interculturally competent individuals to succeed and which protects them from extreme psychological consequences"[3]. Therefore, it is evident that acculturated Latinxs have tools that are allowing them to succeed and cope with acculturative stressors. Research shows that the ability to balance cultures, the ability to speak both languages fluently, perseverance, and optimism in the face of difficulties are tools that are benefiting the mental health and wellbeing of this group. The next section looks at the circumstances of less acculturated Latinxs in the US.

Less Acculturated Latinxs

Unfortunately, my research came to find that there is a massive group of Latinxs missing out on the benefits of mental health interventions and hygiene practices, such as mindfulness and meditation. In 1996, authors Fuertes and Westbrook used the Social, Attitudinal, Familial and Environmental (S.A.F.E) scale to measure the acculturation stress of Hispanics in the United States. They invited 141 Hispanic college students to complete a demographic form that was constructed with three open-ended questions intended to allow the respondents to elaborate on the stress they experienced in the United States, grouped by generational status: early immigrants, late immigrants, and first-generation citizens. Once the scales were analyzed, they found four integral aspects of acculturation stress: domains of family, social and interpersonal relationships, the environment, and society[1]. The findings from the same article found that "[d]ifficulties in communicating and comprehending the English language and difficulties in developing a sense of 'home' in the United States, can exacerbate feelings of loneliness and alienation for the late-immigrant Hispanic students"[1]. These findings came t show that those Latinxs on the other side of the spectrum are indeed affected by acculturative stressors.

The groups studied in Fuertes & Westbrook[1] were defined as "early immigrants--Hispanic students who arrived in the United States before the age of 12, late immigrants--Hispanic students who arrived in the United States after the age of 12, and first-generation citizens--Hispanic students who were born in the United States to foreign-born parents"[1]. The research found that group affected the most by acculturative stress was the late-immigrant Latinxs[1]. Hence, the decision to choose this group for this project.

Nadeem, Lange, Edge, Fongwa, Belin, and Miranda[2] conducted a study "amongst poor African American and Latina young women [and] found that stigma is related to a lower desire to seek treatment, but only among immigrant women, not those who were US born"[2]. Again, this points towards the late-immigrant group of Latinx in need.

Furthermore, the biggest group within Latinx immigrants are from Mexican descent, and research has shown that "Mexicans who were less acculturated had very low use of any services that might address mental health problems, either in the specialty mental health sector or in general human services"[2]. As the author, I can also attest from personal experience that late-immigrant Latinx, like myself, experience struggles and pain due to language barriers, inability to build friendships, feelings of not being home, and being perceived by others as antisocial due to the cultural and language barriers[1].

Torres, Driscoll, and Voell[3] reviewed the effects of the inability to adapt to the dominant culture by identifying acculturative stressors; "**Acculturative stresso**rs can include the pressures of learning a new language, balancing differing cultural values, and having to broker between American and Latino ways of daily living"[3]. All these plus developing a sense of belonging are the main stressors faced by late-immigrant Latinxs, like me; therefore these areas are targeted in the creative project section.

Socioeconomic Status and Social Mobility of Immigrant Latinx

Another big factor in defining the audience for this program was looking at the socioeconomic status (SES) of Latinx immigrants. Rios-Salas and Larson[1] research focused on investigating "the association between discrimination (societal and interpersonal) and mental health (depressive symptoms and self-esteem) among Latino adolescents with recent immigration histories, and test how this association differs by parental socioeconomic status"[1]. The findings from this study suggest that "higher parental SES may be protective in situations of discrimination, but not necessarily in all situations. In fact, relatively higher SES among Latino adolescents with recent immigration histories may be associated with worse mental health"[1].

Another factor considered in the audience selection was social mobility. Social mobility refers to the "movement of individuals, families, or groups through a system of social hierarchy or stratification…[if] the move involves a change in social class, it is called 'vertical mobility' and involves either 'upward mobility' or 'downward mobility'."[2]. A recent study by Mendoza, Armbrister, and Abraído-Lanza[3] precisely explored this area, and the research focused on "how changes in social mobility from the country of origin to the U.S. may relate to Latina women's health care interactions… [it] examined the association among social mobility and self-rated health, quality of care, and medical mistrust"[3]. In this study, the authors came to find that "[d]ownward social mobility was associated with more years of education, fewer years lived in the U.S., and greater medical mistrust compared to stable or upward social mobility, while upward social mobility associated significantly with more years lived in the U.S. compared to downward and stable social mobility"[3]. This research comes to show that there is a high possibility that recent more educated immigrants have higher mistrust and fewer chances of engaging in mental or health care practices designed for the mainstream. Due to these finding, personal understanding, and the level of comprehension need for the creative project, I decided to target college-educated bilingual Latinxs.

Mindfulness and Meditation Versus Conventional Interventions for Coping with Acculturative Stress

According to Torres, Driscoll, and Voell[1] and Torres[2], acculturative stress triggers revolve around four aspects: Immigration circumstances, the ability to balance and negotiate different cultural values, the ability to learn a new language, and mastering the ability to battle feelings of isolation and not belonging. From personal experience with these scenarios, I primarily believe that mindfulness and meditation can help with dealing and coping with these stressors. This decision was solidified by the scientific-proof of the Mindfulness-Based Stress Reduction Programs' (MBSR) ability to teach people how to manage stress. On the website of the Center for Mindfulness at the University of

Massachusetts Medical School, it states that Dr. Jon Kabat-Zinn founded the Stress Reduction Program in 1979 to help participants learn "how to use their innate resources and abilities to respond more effectively to stress, pain, and illness"[3]

Lastly, research from Bernal, Jiménez-Chafey and Domenech-Rodríguez[4] highlighted the need for culturally-attuned interventions. It shared that "Cultural adaptation has not focused on the 'systematic modification of an evidence-based treatment or interventions protocol to consider language, culture, and context in such a way that it is compatible with the client's cultural patterns, meanings, and values'"[4]. Therefore, research like this one inspired me to explore migration circumstances, backgrounds, and traditions, along with traditional sayings (*dichos*) along the guidebook, in order to bring a sense of sensitivity to Latinx diversity. Let me emphasize that throughout the guidebook the reader is never discouraged from attending conventional treatment; instead, they are encouraged to lose fear and learn more about mental health care and hygiene. This guidebook, in a way, is a stepping stone into mental health care for Latinx immigrants in the United States.

Mindfulness and Meditation

Before continuing the argument to introduce mindfulness and meditation practices as a way to cope with the acculturative stress and feelings of not belonging of Latinx late-immigrants, it is essential to know the basic concepts of mindfulness and meditation, so there is a clear understanding of what these practices entail.

The most popular definition in the western world for mindfulness is the one from Jon Kabat-Zinn[1]; he describes mindfulness as the "moment-to-moment, non-judgmental awareness, cultivated by paying attention in a specific way, that is, in the present moment, and as non-reactively, as non-judgmental, and as open-heartedly as possible"[1]. Furthermore, Kirmayer[2] wrote a paper considering the meanings of mindfulness meditation in a cultural context[2]. He describes Mindfulness as a "form of awareness [that] is assumed to have intrinsic value in promoting positive mental health and adaptation by interrupting discursive thoughts that give rise to suffering"[2]. In the same paper, the authors clarify that mindfulness is currently erroneously promoted as a way to achieve happiness in life, and this is something this project is not intending to do. This guidebook intends to help cope and heal acculturative stress by educating the reader and inviting the reader to reflect and practice culturally-attuned mindfulness and meditation practices.

Meditation, as defined by Salzberg[3], consists of, "esencialmente en entrenar a nuestra atención para que podemos ser más conscientes no solo de nuestros propios mecanismos internos, sino también de lo que ocurre a nuestro alrededor en el aquí y el ahora" ("of training our attention so we can be more conscious of our internal world, and what happens around us in the here and now")[3]. Salzberg[3] continues to explain that meditation can be practiced in many ways: silence and stillness, using our voice and sound, or moving our bodies; all the techniques have the same goal of training the mind to pay attention[3]. Furthermore, Julie Brefczynski-Lewis[4] defines meditation as "a family of mental training practices that are designed to familiarize the practitioner with specific types of mental processes"[4]. In this guidebook, the reader learns varied culturally-attuned meditation practices that follow along with the main topic of the week.

Mindfulness practices.

In mindfulness practices, one exercises acceptance of mental states (thoughts), emotions, and body; one works with training the mind to focus and see clearly without being swept by rumination, worries, plans, daydreaming, body-pain and aches, or other distractions. Gethin[1] explains that this activity "requires remembering one's purpose in meditating, in terms of ethical and spiritual goals of eliminating greed, hatred, and delusion while cultivating wisdom, compassion, and loving kindness"[1]. In mindfulness practice, we become aware of the mental, emotional and physical sensations and happenings that manifest in our mental, physical, and emotional states; it is the role of the meditator who understands mindfulness to become the observer and become aware and embracive of whatever state is present in the body, mind, and heart. Through this place of observation and insight or analysis, the meditator can try to introduce new wholesome ways of relating to negative and uncomfortable states of mind, body, and heart.

More specifically, the observation practiced during mindfulness practices focuses on learning about oneself, through *vipassana* or 'insight' meditation. In this type of meditation, as Goldstein[1] explains one is "learning to focus attention on the breath while simply observing any sensations, thoughts, or feelings that arise"[1]. Tan[2] explains it in a similarly simple way,

> Mindfulness trains two important faculties, attention and meta-attention. Attention is something we all understand. William James has a very nice definition for it: 'taking possession by the mind, in clear and vivid form'…meta-attention is the ability to know that your attention has wandered away.[2]

Mindfulness or awareness of the different things happening in our subjective and bodily experience can be practiced in varied ways, as we have learned. Each week the guidebook covers new ways to apply culturally-attuned mindfulness practices.

Healing Acculturative Stress of Late-immigrant Latinxs in the United States

It is crucial to provide an explanation of the area of mental health that this guidebook attempts to serve. Therefore, this guidebook approaches mental health hygiene practices from Dr. Dan Siegel's perspective and definition of the mind as the subjective experience.

In a lecture titled *Mindfulness, Mindsight and the Brain: What is Mind and Mental Health,* Dr. Daniel Siegel[1] starts by addressing a few synonyms of the psyche commonly used by psychologists and psychotherapists; the synonyms mentioned for the mind were the soul, the spirit, and the intellect. Dr. Siegel challenges the standard definition that "the mind is what the brain does;" he redefines the mind as a lived texture, a 'we' sense, the individual moments in our lives, the nature of subjective experience in each of us. In other words, this subjective experience is that voice in our head that holds our beliefs, our perceptions, our intentions, and the meanings behind our narratives.

Dr. Siegel highlights that the ability to focus is a critical aspect in creating meaningful and long-lasting relationships and that the science of relationship shows that people who have their subjective experiences tuned up by others do better in life. In the same video conference, Dr. Siegel[1] defines this subjective experience as the feeling of emotion, the texture of thought, the beliefs we have, the perceptions we hold, the intentions that go through us, and the meanings embedded in our narratives. This approach and definition is emphasized in week one of the guidebook. The goal is to allow participants to start understanding what is happening inside of them.

Kirmayer[2] along with cited work from Williams and Kabat-Zinn does an excellent job of explaining the universality of mindfulness that is a crucial component that makes this practice helpful for Latinx late-immigrants facing acculturative stress and feelings of not belonging.

Since Buddhist meditative practices are concerned with embodied awareness and the cultivation of clarity, emotional balance (equanimity) and compassion, and since these capacities can be refined and developed via the honing and intentional deployment of attention, the roots of Buddhist meditation practices are de facto universal. This universalism is consistent with Buddhist teachings and supports the conviction that the practice of mindfulness meditation—while it may need to be adapted to meet the needs of specific kinds of personalities or cultures—can lead to the same insights into the nature of mind for practitioners in any context.[2]

From this statement, it becomes clear that the core of all human beings does not differ from one another; however, in the process of working with specific communities, it is beneficial to create practices that resonate with the specific group. For example, one of the mindfulness practices presented in the guidebook is called Ancestral Greeting by Juana Bordas, and it was included in the guidebook because when I practiced, it gave a sense of appreciation, connection, and understanding of my ancestors and my heritage. So I hope the reader can also benefit from the wisdom, guidance, and energy deeply rooted in ourselves. Another sample is one of the meditations developed by me, it is titled

'My accent is my unique stamp in the world'. This guided meditation helps the listener connect with their uniqueness in a compassionate way.

It has been a joy to be able to use research and personal experience to develop mindfulness and meditation practices that embrace culture and history. In this process, it was important to think about social context, "[t]hese contexts include modernity, mass migration, and the global networks and economic systems that work to exacerbate our appetites, amplify inequalities, impair adaptation, and constrain moral action"[2]. The reflective questions take a significant role in inviting the reader to consider their own social context throughout the process of healing and coping with acculturative stress. The overall hope is to allow each reader to advance at their pace, and work with what feels right at each moment.

Considerations for Guidebook Development

This section focuses on the research considered in the creation, development, and completion of this culturally-attuned mindfulness and meditation guidebook.

Acknowledgment of Mental Health Stigmas

The Latinx community carries within a heavy list of mental health stigmas, which can affect the engagement of this population in mental health care or hygiene. It is important for participants to understand what stigma is, where these stigmas are generating from, and how they can overcome these stigmas. If participants do not acknowledge and work with overcoming mental health stigmas, these hidden blockages can take a toll on their practice and the effectiveness of the program.

Fripp and Carlson[1], defined mental health stigmas as the internalization of stereotypes or discriminatory behavior toward others; their paper specifically explored the influence of attitude and stigma on mental health care participation in the Latinx and African American populations. Fripp and Carlson[1] explained that negative experiences could be manifested through the actions and attitude from the practitioner treating the individual, his/her family members, or social influences[1]. Furthermore, the paper explained that "[t]he way a provider views mental health issues, the way society views mental health, or the way individuals view their issues all contribute to the decision-making process related to treatment enrollment"[1]. As shown in this research, it is not easy to overcome stigmas in just one training or conversation. However, this project hopes that each reader can start to work on acknowledging, reflecting and overcoming hidden or present personal, social, and cultural stigmas.

Craft, Crone, DeLeon, and Ajayi[2] define "[m]ental health stigma [as] a negative evaluation of those with mental illness or of mental health treatment"[2]. Their study focused on perceived and personal mental health stigmas in Latinx and African American college students. Their paper broke down the origin of stigmas in two main sources: "perceived and personal"[2]. Both are further explained as follows,

> [p]erceived stigma concerns negative attitudes where one believes that society as a whole holds about individuals with mental illness, while personal stigma focuses on one's own beliefs about individuals with mental illness. Mental health stigma, particularly personal stigma, is important because those who hold stigma beliefs are less willing to obtain the needed treatment.[2]

The method used in this paper to organize stigmas inspired the content and explanations of week four in the guidebook. The classification also takes into consideration research from Guarnaccia, Martinez, and Acosta[3], who "organized [mental health stigmas] into several dimensions: provider barriers, barriers in the service system, community-level barriers, barriers in the social networks of people in the community, and person-centered barriers"[3]. In their report, they list some of the barriers, which include health insurance, language barriers, discrimination from the system, and lack of information about services in language. More specifically they highlighted the effect that rooted family and community stigmas have towards the individual concerning mental illnesses; additionally, person-centered barriers included lack of recognition of mental health problems, the stigma of mental illness, and a determined attitude. They also identified that the lack of health insurance and citizenship/immigration status were major barriers to mental health participation[3].

As mentioned, the project groups these barriers and stigmas into two categories: Family-community generated and self-generated. The Family-community section includes perceived stigmas generated from outside sources such as health providers, the system, society, and social network. Self-generated considerations revolve around person-centered or personal belief-based stigmas. The next sections expand on these groups, and explain how the guidebook serves as a stepping stone into developing healthier relationships with mental hygiene, and this emphasis can hopefully have long-term effects on higher acceptance and engagement in conventional mental health care from Latinx late-immigrants in the US.

Family-community generated mental health stigmas.

The Latinx culture is considered a highly collectivist society, and in this type of societal bond, "the core unit is the group; societies exist, and individuals must fit into them. Individuals are seen as fundamentally connected and related through relationships and group memberships"[1]. Because of this importance, *familismo* is highlighted in this section. Carteret[2] explains that in familism there is a tendency to be highly group-oriented, and "[a] strong emphasis is placed on family as the major source of one's identity and protection against the hardships of life"[2]. This trait is further discussed in the cultural values section; however, it is important to associate it with stigmas because it provides a better understanding of how family culture can impact engagement in mental hygiene or care.

Because of the importance given to family, it is common for Latinxs in mental distress to reach out within their areas of comfort, as gathered in various research from Akincigil, Mayers, and Fulghum, 2011; Brinson and Kottler, 1995; Cabassa and Zayas, 2007; Hovey and King, 1996; and Guarnaccia, Martinez, and Acosta, 2005.

Latino Americans traditionally endorse a collectivistic perspective and often seek assistance within their ethnic enclave for sources of support (family, clergy) before pursuing clinical care. A core component of collectivism includes a focus on *familismo*, which refers to the strong identification and attachment to one's family, placing emphasis on the needs of the family over the individual. Given the Latino emphasis on family, Latinos may be more resistant to seeking treatment because of the shame they fear it will bring on themselves as well as their families.[3]

This strong communal sense of society leads Latinxs to use communion and the church as a safe place to express their distress without putting their worries, issues and suffering out in public. García-Campayo, Demarzo, Shonin, and Van Gordon[4] further explain that for Latinxs "the need to conform to social norms can increase the risk of manipulation or feelings of responsibility"[4]. Even though these are socially embedded behaviors, they generate internal or personal stigmas and negative attitudes that may be filled with feelings and thoughts of shame and distress. The guidebook strongly emphasizes the dissociation of church and meditation, it also works a lot with the identification of negative mental patterns and behaviors that cause distress. More specifically, the content in week one establishes building a healthy relationship with the subjective experience, followed by work in trying to understand the cause of stress and how it manifests in our lives. These tools can slowly start reshaping these perspectives around self-blame and shame of needing mental health guidance. Shame is further explored in week seven of the guidebook.

As seen in research, religious affiliations have a substantial effect on the decision-making process for Latinxs, and this is mainly related to the beliefs that distress may be coming from stronger forces outside of them; therefore, strong religious affiliations lead Latinxs to blame suffering on faith. As expressed by Alvarez and Satcher[3], "Latinos holding religious or traditional spiritual beliefs may attribute psychological distress to supernatural forces, explaining why they are less likely to utilize mental health services"[3]. The process of overcoming this stigma is led through education on mental health throughout the guidebook. Through the cultivation of knowledge, the hope is that the readers recognize for themselves that supernatural forces outside their control do not cause psychological distress.

Bravo[4] cites the work of Bermúdez, Kirkpatrick, Hecker, and Torre-Robles; these authors name fatalism as the source of resistance to mental health care outside the church. The same authors describe fatalism "as the feeling that everything occurs because their god wills it and that it is ultimately out of their control"[4]. The Latinx culture carries with it a sense of loss of control and ownership of their mental health and wellbeing because they link it with faith and supernatural forces. The goal is that the reflections, concepts, and practices presented in the guidebook can awaken the reader to realize and see that his mental health and well-being can be under their control.

Turner and Llamas[3] state that "[i]t is possible that those with a stronger spirituality may turn to a religious or spiritual leader rather than going to therapy"[3]. Even more, the same authors agree that younger generations are still affected by these strong religious ties, and, as stated in the paper, "[i]t appears that among Latino college students spiritual beliefs play an important role in the decision to seek mental health treatment"[3]. Religion ties and spirituality are big bridges as well as barriers to mental health practices. The hope is that readers and participants can understand that religion and spirituality can both act as bridges to mental health care and hygiene; through personal reflection sections, the readers can start to question existing predisposed mindsets curiously.

Other than formalized religion, there is also a widespread use of folk treatments to treat mental distress and mental illnesses. Research from Satcher[3] states that "Latinos may utilize spiritual and traditional healing practices such as seeking *curanderos* (folk healers). It is estimated that as high as 44% of Latinos use alternative treatment approaches"[3]. For example, for Cubans in Miami, it is more common and culturally acceptable to treat their mental health with *santeria* and

179

espiritismo, instead of using traditional mental health care[4]. It seems more culturally accepted and less stigmatized to attend alternative care instead of seeing a mental health professional. In week three and six, mindfulness is emphasized as an alternative form of mental health hygiene. The hope is that by using popular terms and practices, people can lose fear and open to learning these practices.

In week four, the guidebook addresses the fact that many Latinx women have the unconsciously ingrained attitude that good behavior for women is to portray purity and sanctity, referred to as *Marianismo* (Marianism). Comas-Diaz[4] defined it as the "gender role in which women of the Latinx community are expected to maintain characteristics similar to the Virgin Mary. This entails maintaining virginity, both physically and spiritually, as well as being selfless, unadulterated, docile, and coy"[4]. Additionally, this attitude and culturally embedded role refer to "the high-value Latino women place on being dedicated, loving, and supportive wives and mothers"[2]. These deep cultural beliefs are factors that keep some women from participating in mental health hygiene. The pressure to maintain this role of perfection and sanctity within their communities and families is detrimental to engagement in mental health hygiene. Again, education is key in overcoming these type of stigmas and barriers; stigmas are intensely worked on in week four if the guidebook.

Another factor that affects mental health engagement of Latinxs is discrimination. Due to the clash of the universal culture with the varied Latinx cultures present in the United States, discrimination is highly experienced in the Latinx community. The diversity of cultures includes varied sets of beliefs, behaviors, and idioms. In a study visited about the role of therapy fears, Ethnic identity, and spirituality on access to mental health treatment among Latinx college students, Corble-Smith, Thomas, and St. George[3] emphasized that "Systemic variables can include experiences of discrimination and racism, which can result from ethnic/racial biases against Latinos. Latinos are also more likely to distrust the health care systems due to past discriminatory experiences"[3]. The second main topic of this guidebook under acculturative stress is belonging. Throughout the guidebook, the participants are learning about belonging to themselves, their families, and communities. The goal is to create a coping tool and antidote to discrimination. By teaching readers about who they are, where they come from, and the interconnectedness of the world, there is a hope that pride, compassion, and love can rein in their hearts. Therefore, this new way of seeing and being can help diminish feelings of not belonging and feeling discriminated.

Caldwell and Karcher[4] explain that in Western cultures there is a high tendency to put down those who have the "wrong skin color, wrong hair, wrong eyes, wrong body parts, wrong way of walking, etc."[4]. This statement shows that what is different from the universal culture, such as the way someone looks, talks, or behaves, can create a perfect environment for discrimination. Latinxs are then predisposed with fear of being discriminated against, and these experiences can bring susceptibility when seeking help. Latinxs need to become aware that they may not fit in the norm because of accents, broken English, minority race, and different cultures, but this should not keep them from belonging. Becoming aware can be beneficial to embracing our roots and opening to the new mainstream culture. Embracing and celebrating our differences, traditions, ancestry, race, culture, and uniqueness can make a huge impact on dealing and healing from discrimination.

Furthermore, another externally generated barrier in getting mental health is having access to health benefits, as explained by Casas and Keefe, and Chavez and Torres's research[5], the "[l]ack of health benefits in the jobs and industries where Mexican immigrants are concentrated, the high cost of services and relatively low wages, pressures of work, and legal status issues all act as barriers to service utilization"[5]. Studies reviewed in the same paper by Guarnaccia, Martinez, and Acosta's[5] remarks that the Mexican community is the one that uses services the least due to "[l]ack of health insurance and language barriers...Immigrants are even less likely to use mental health services than U.S. born Latinos"[5]. The 'Mental health in the Hispanic immigrant community report' led by Guarnaccia, Martinez and Acosta in 2005 led to the conclusion "that for some Latinos, when cultural, linguistic and financial barriers are removed or lessened, rates of utilization of outpatient mental health services increase significantly"[5]. As explained in the guidebook description, readers who are students, unemployed, or from low-income are encouraged to apply to participate in the online sessions at no cost or discounted cost. The goal is to make this project accessible to Latinx in need.

All Latinxs migrate from countries with different political, economic, and social circumstances, and these differences create "[a]nother barrier within the mental health field [which is] is a lack of extensive multicultural training and Spanish-speaking clinicians, impacting the clinician's ability to provide culturally appropriate services to Latino students"[3]. Similarly, as explained by Rios-Ellis[6], "Latino/a Americans are faced with the challenge of identifying practitioners within their community who are not only competent but are able to provide bilingual or monolingual Spanish-speaking counseling services"[6]. The guidebook has taken the diversity within the Latinx immigrants very seriously throughout the book. There are *dichos* (sayings) from all Latin American countries; also, there are diversity-filled illustrations through the guidebook.

Language fluency varies according to each's migration history and circumstances. As explored in Guarnaccia, Martinez & Acosta[5] research "[l]anguage barriers also figure prominently in Latino's use of mental health services. A large proportion of the Latino population in the U.S. speaks Spanish as their primary language, though this differs among the major Latino groups and across studies (in part, depending on how fully they include undocumented individuals)"[5]. So even within in-language services in the Latinx culture, there are cultural differences that can affect the care. Particularly in the same area of language lies the "[l]ack of information about where to seek mental health services can also be a barrier, particularly lack of information in Spanish. Given that most mental health services are offered in separate settings from general medical services, it is not always clear even to the general population where to get these services"[5]. The long-term goal is to offer this guidebook in Spanish, so it can be accessible to those who have not been able to learn English fluently yet. For now, the guidebook includes sources for Latinx culturally-attuned Mental Health Services.

Additionally, when mainstream mental health does become available, many practitioners are not aware of idioms and expressions wrongly but commonly used for describing mental health symptoms and distress by Latinxs,

Recognition of the idioms of *nervios* and *ataque de nervios* as important signs of psychological distress among many Puerto Ricans, especially those from working class and poor backgrounds, can contribute to the recognition of psychosocial problems in primary care. At the same time, there are not simple translations of these idioms of distress into psychiatric diagnoses; rather they cut across a range of distress and disorder requiring careful assessment of both the symptoms and contexts of experience.[5]

At the end of the guidebook there is a list of mental health idioms and definitions commonly used by Latinxs, these may help those Latinxs that may have trouble relating with English stress related mental terminology.

Self-generated mental health stigmas.

Self-generated fear, barriers, and stigmas are strongly connected to family-community generated ones; however, within these internal factors mainly reside personal responsibility or a sense of culpability and responsibility for what is happening. Craft, Crone, DeLeon, and Ajayi[1] explain that "[c]ommon stigma beliefs include that those with mental illness are dangerous, will not recover and that their mental illness is their own fault"[1]. The same authors found that "[a]n examination of a Latino sample noted that individuals who desire social distance from those with mental illness were more likely to seek treatment"[1]. Personal responsibility extends this fear of being isolated or rejected within their community, and as highlighted in research by Corrigan and Matthews[2], "if a person is fearful of being stigmatized, he or she will be reluctant to attend mental health services to avoid prejudicial treatment within the systems he or she encounters"[2]. Based on personal experience, I created this guidebook as a tool that can be practiced in solitude, and the privacy and safety of home, because self-generated fear was one of the biggest barriers on my path to wellbeing and mental health hygiene practice.

In the same realm of personal responsibility, guilt also comes into play; "Health-related guilt appears to be more common in Latin countries (e.g., feeling guilty about being depressed or being diagnosed with an illness)"[3]. Additionally, the same paper explains that "Latin patients can be less eager to know the intricate details of their illness, or to engage with decisions on diagnosis and treatment"[3]. Latinxs carry a huge burden by taking personal responsibility for attempting to portray good mental health even if it is not the case. The option to read the guidebook and participate in an online session can help Latinxs cope with some of these barriers. Also, the cultivation and understanding of self-compassion in week four can help with battling these feelings of guilt and responsibility. As research had shown that most Latinxs,

> felt they should be able to cope with mental health problems themselves [and] were less likely to seek care, even when they reported symptoms indicative of mental illness. This self-reliant attitude was recently expressed in a focus group of Latinos in Spanish as *ponerse de su parte* (contributing one's part). This attitude reflects the feeling that one should be strong enough to cope with life's problems on their own and with the help of family and not need to depend on the mental health system.[4]

Most of these fears around mental health were reduced for me with the proper education and training. It is my hope, as the author, that this guidebook can help many people suffering in silence.

Another issue is that "[w]hen Latinos do seek help for mental health problems, they are more likely to do so in the general medical sector than in specialty mental health services"[4]. As it happened to me, I actually did not have a primary care doctor; I only had a gynecologist whom I visited for women's checkup routines. In my ignorance, I encountered discomfort and awkwardness when I expressed my worries about my mental health. I have learned that in order to lower this misconception, it is important to educate my community on mental health care and services. Therefore, the guidebook includes an appendix listing

Stress-related Idioms in Latinx Community, plus another referencing to Latinx Culturally-attuned Mental Health Services.

Craft, Crone, DeLeon, and Ajayi[1] emphasize this importance on education, "One of the most well-researched factors related to understanding mental health stigma for ethnic minorities is lack of knowledge"[1]. Furthermore, the same authors explain that poor knowledge of mental health disorders can be the primary cause of fear or anxiety about mental illness[1]. Something that is impactful is that the actual word 'mental health' carries the most powerful stigma because it highlights the field of the unknown, Jenkins highlights that the use of idioms such as,

> the label of *locura* or madness carries strong negative connotations. Someone who is *loco* is seen as severely mentally ill, potentially violent and incurable. Labeling a family member with mental illness as suffering from *nervios* serves to destigmatize that person's experience both in the family and the community.[4]

Again, the emphasis on explaining mental health and distress is shown throughout the book, and week four strongly focuses on acknowledging and educating on stigmas.

Heavy stigmas are also found around the use of medication to treat mental illness, "Among Latinos, beliefs about mental health treatment included that antidepressants were related to ideas about being 'crazy' or associated with illegal drug use"[1]. Furthermore, "Latinos appear to have significant concerns about psychotropic medications. These include both the strength and the addictive potential of those medications"[4]. Multiple times the guidebook discloses encouragement to seek out professional help if the reader or participant is experiencing

186

strong and unmanageable symptoms of distress. Also, as the author, I disclose my own fears and stigmas with the hope that it will help eliminate some of the fears, barriers, and stigmas present in the reader or participant.

Cultural Competence

This project looks to specifically serve the Latinx community of bilingual late-immigrants in the United States and because of this uniqueness, I believe, that cultural competencies should be a priority. Cultural competence is a learned behavior that takes in consideration beliefs, attitudes, knowledge, and skills from individuals, and "[i]t is typically defined as an 'active process, that is ongoing…that never reaches an endpoint', that takes into consideration the complexity of the client's diversity, acknowledges limitations, and the need to always improve. Other terms like 'cultural sensitivity' and 'cultural awareness' are often used synonymously"[1]. The book includes illustrations that take into consideration the diversity of the people reading it; the exercises also consider the variety of cultures within the Latinx immigrants in the US.

Another way to understand Cultural Competence is by seeing it as a type of empathetic role; Golonka Carmichael[1] puts it as having "willingness to 'sit in the fire', so to speak, and proactively approach the uncomfortable experiences of verbal and nonverbal communication and expression. This is not merely a skill or technique, but an adapted life choice. As such, some traditional principles may need modification or further development"[1]. The guidebook offers some of my personal story and struggles; the purpose is to allow the reader to connect and identify at some level with me. Also, the option for participants to join an online class is encouraged. And the purpose of this is to create an environment where they can build an empathetic connection with me and other students going through similar experiences.

Angel and Guarnaccia, Guarnaccia et al., Lewis-Fernandez, Liebowitz et al., and Escobar et al. come to agree and explain that,

> Latinos tend to be very expressive of their physical and emotional pain, often through rich somatic idioms. This 'somatization' of distress is misunderstood as either hypochondriasis or a lack of ability to express the psychological dimensions of emotional distress–neither of which is accurate. Rather Latinos express depression and anxiety through a mix of physical and emotional complaints.[2]

The process of teaching and educating on mindfulness of the body, thoughts, and emotions has the goal to help Latinxs find new avenues to express their acculturative distress. In the guidebook, it is clear that I am not a certified therapist, psychologist, or psychotherapist. Instead, I am represented as a Latinx late-immigrant who overcame mental distress and someone that embraces any type of mental health hygiene and care practice.

It is not easy to find a quick fix that can serve this diverse group perfectly, but it is important to take the right steps that can start helping in the development of tools and services that can serve at least a portion of this growing minority. Torres'[3] study focused on two things "(a) to discover and generate themes regarding the skills Latinos deem as necessary for successful intercultural interactions and (b) to derive a cultural model of Latino intercultural competence based on these emergent characteristics"[3]. Therefore, this research focused on revealing the traits and qualities found in Latinxs who can successfully navigate as immigrants in the United States, "[t]he most prominent theme in the cultural model of Latino intercultural competence involved Ambition and Desire to Succeed. This characteristic involved the ability to have realistic goals about living within two different cultures and continuing to strive for more despite the current circumstances"[3]. In other words, the ability to find a balance between two cultures shows cultural competence and therefore can predict professional success for Latinx immigrants in the United States. The work from week two on connecting to personal story, ancestry, and roots hopes to awaken the sense of interconnectedness; this sense can help in working with symptoms of acculturative stress.

Cultural Values

This guidebook works a lot with concepts of belonging and with positively embracing heritage, cultural values, and traditions. The reason is that from my personal experience, and the reviewed research, it is evident that those who honor and are knowledgeable about their past are better able to find a good and healthy balance between cultures. Torres[1] explains that "a key aspect of cultural success involved having pride in the Latino culture and keeping up with cultural traditions and values"[1]. Personally, celebrating traditional festivities along with new American festivities has kept my heart fulfilled and close to what truly matters to me. Therefore, Miville et al's[2] cultural values are addressed throughout the guidebook and help show respect and value for each's story, traditions, and heritage.

Therefore, this guidebook takes into consideration Miville et al's[2] general set of values associated with succeeding in engagement from the Latinx culture. The values highlighted included "*colectivismo, familismo, simpatía, confianza, respeto, fatalismo, and personalismo*"[2]. The guidebook hopes to have addressed all of them throughout the content and practices.

The first value is *Colectivismo* (collectivism), in collectivism "[i]ndividuals are typically defined by interpersonal connections, relationships, and group membership"[2]. Latin American cultures fall within this context, in contrast to the US mainstream culture which can be considered more of an individualistic culture; as explained by Oyserman and Lee[4] "the core unit is the individual; societies exist to promote the well-being of individuals. Individuals are seen as separate from one another and as the basic unit of analysis"[4]. Late-immigrant Latinxs tend to have higher ties to a collectivistic mindset, where everyone is connected and related[4]. The guidebook serves this value by dedicating two weeks of content to work with family, ancestry, and interconnectedness with the world. Also, the mindfulness practices presented each week involve exercises that ask the participants to connect with others in their family and friendship circles. Lastly, the reader is encouraged to connect with an online class to follow along with readings.

The second one is *Familismo* (familyism), it "emphasizes the role and influence of the family, which is broadly defined to include nuclear and extended family members as well as close friends...Familismo is often associated with interdependence, obligation, loyalty, solidarity, and reciprocity"[2] defines it as "[t]he term Latinos use to describe their supreme collective loyalty to extended family"[2]. Bermúdez, Kirkpatrick, Hecker, and Torres-Robles[3] describe it as "a cultural value and belief that the family is central in the life of the individual. It is thought to be the basis of the Cuban family structure, the Mexican–American family structure, the Puerto Rican family structure, and the Central and South American family structure"[3]. Research from the same authors also came to find that "Latinos are more likely to emphasize the group over the individual"[3]. Each week the reflection questions take into consideration the influence of family. Also, the mindfulness exercises revolve around the importance of family and friends for Latinx.

The third value is *Personalismo* (Personification), and it emphasizes the importance of having smooth interpersonal relationships through warm, friendly, and personal interactions"[1]. Furthermore, Personification can also be understood as the "[f]ormal yet personal connections expressed through language, structure, and interactions are conduits to respect the role of each person within the collective"[2]. Bermúdez, Kirkpatrick, Hecker, and Torres-Robles[3] explain that in *personalismo* "Latinos define their self-worth by their inner qualities that give them self-respect, an inner sense of dignity, and the ability to earn the respect of others"[3]. In weeks six and seven there is an emphasis in the practice of compassion and empathy, which fall along this value. Also, the illustrations and personal narrative are there to serve in creating this sense of personal connection. The optional online session can also help in connecting at a deeper and more meaningful level.

The fourth value is *Simpatía* (Kindness). It "refers to the Latina/o cultural value that each individual carries a responsibility to advance harmonious relationships through behaviors that communicate mutual respect, emphasize positives, and deemphasize negatives to achieve smooth interpersonal exchanges"[2]. Another way to understand this is as the "emphasis on politeness and pleasantness even in the face of stress"[5]. The language used in the content, mindfulness exercises, illustrations, guided meditations, cultural sayings, and optional online class consider this. The hope is to offer kindness to the reader and participant so they can connect openly, freely, and non- judgmentally, hence the use of the inclusive term Latinx.

The fifth value is *Confianza* (trust). In this value, individuals are invested in establishing relationships based on reciprocal trust. With *confianza*, individuals can comfortably express their deepest fears, wishes, and intimacies with an inner circle of close friends and colleagues. Essentially, *confianza* fosters and ensures a reciprocal process whereby individuals' best interests are prioritized, pursued, and preserved[2]. The addition of my personal story into the guidebook was because of this; I wanted to create a sense of relatedness, connection, and trust.

The sixth one is *Respeto* (respect). When someone refers to respect in Latinx culture, it means that it "is expected in interpersonal relationships for *confianza* to be accorded. The expression *'Me faltó el respeto'* indicates an interpersonal breach, perhaps in the form of a micro aggression, that cannot be ignored to maintain authentic, equitable, and reciprocal relationships"[2]. Carteret[5] also provides a definition of *respeto* meaning "that each person is expected to defer to those who are in a position of authority because of age, gender, social position, title, economic status, etc. Healthcare providers, and doctors especially, are viewed as authority figures"[5].

Additionally, *respeto* "is considered a core personality trait that reflects the values and functions of interdependence, obedience, passivity, and control of aggression"[3]. This value is integrated in a passive voice throughout the guidebook by allowing the participants to work with things at a personal level, allowing them to write on their journal, and providing optional sharing practices. The option of sharing experiences and thoughts gives room for privacy and respect. The language and activities try to comply at best with this value.

The seventh value is *Fatalismo* (fatalism). Fatalism "emphasizes the 'here and now' and tends to promote an external locus of control. The *dicho* (saying) *"El hombre propone y Dios dispone"* (Man proposes, and God disposes of) characterizes this value of relinquishing false notions of control. Fatalism is typically associated with religiosity or spirituality and involves individuals turning to, trusting in, and surrendering to God's will, a higher power, or external forces[2]. Carteret[5] describes this behavior as "a strong belief that uncertainty is inherent in life and each day is taken as it comes...belief that the individual can do little to alter fate"[5]. Bermúdez, Kirkpatrick, Hecker, and Torres-Robles[3] further explain in their research that fatalism is "a belief among Latinos that some things are meant to be regardless of the individual's intervention. Latinos traditionally have had a strong sense of destiny and a belief in divine providence governing the world. Major life events are seen as inevitable and there is a fatalistic attitude that whatever shall be, shall be"[3]. In week three, mindfulness is explained to the reader as a new way to cultivate new perspectives, and, in this section, the concept of fatalism is brought into questioning and reflection. The hope is that through mindful writing and reflections, and specifically from mindfulness practices like *El Trensito* (The train) from week four, the readers can learn to identify fatalistic patterns that may be keeping them from relaxing and belonging to themselves.

Mindfulness and Mindfulness-Based Stress Reduction in Latinx Communities

This section highlights considerations specifically derived from mindfulness and mindfulness-based stress reduction research articles and study trials.

Length of practice.

In 2017, García-Campayo, Demarzo, Shonin, and Van Gordon[1] gained insights from people who had delivered an 8-week Mindfulness-Based Stress Reduction (MBSR) program throughout Latin America. The guidebook is not a version of the MBSR; however, it consider it and resembles it in some areas of work and emphasis. The guidebook takes a lot of the recommendations seriously because the target audience comes from Latin America and this research was extracted from this population. García-Campayo, Demarzo, Shonin, and Van Gordon[1] came to find that "the three most different issues affecting the teaching of mindfulness and compassion in Latin countries, in comparison with the UK and US, are the amount of daily practice (this should probably be shorter for Latins), the role of informal practice and interpersonal mindfulness (more important in Latin environments), and the issue of potential religious influences"[1]. The authors first recommend that meditations times should be modified from 45-minute standards to 20-minute variations, so they fit better with the lifestyle of Latinxs. Therefore, the guidebook weekly meditation practices vary from five to twenty minutes per sitting; time increases as each week advances.

Overall, it is important to mention the research of Crane et al.[2], which focused on identifying what factors are needed to consider a curriculum a truly mindfulness-based program. In their paper, the authors encourage developers to consider variations in program structure, length, and delivery to serve the population and context at hand well[2]. Hence the length of practice adaptations in the guidebook, sitting meditation time varies from 5 – 20 minutes throughout the guidebook. Therefore, most of the length of practice increases as the course advances; however, the students can choose shorter sitting periods to accommodate their life schedules and availability.

Learning methods.

García-Campayo, Demarzo, Shonin, and Van Gordon[1] also highlight that "audio- or video-guided practices seem to be employed more frequently and for longer durations in Latin versus US populations"[1]. The guidebook encourages the option to join an online group and class simultaneously with the guidebook, with the intention to apply critical Latinx cultural values of familyism, collectivism, and personification.

Another suggestion identified was to reduce and adjust the retreat time, as most mindfulness training integrate a 1-full day retreat. For Latin Americans "a full-day retreat requires a significantly greater time commitment (i.e., potentially conflicting with long working hours and social/family commitments). Reducing or eliminating the full-day retreat component may therefore be beneficial"[1]. Similarly, Ortiz[2] provided an MBSR training to Latinxs and found that even with providing financial and physical assistance to families to attend the all-day retreat, participants still found themselves in a position to be unable to attend, due to childcare difficulties[2]. Based on these recommendations, neither the guidebook or the optional online class require the completion of a retreat.

Regarding location and teaching approach, research from Williams, Williams, and Jackson[2] share that "Childcare issues, transportation, work schedules, and financial constraints all present barriers for many minorities to participate in inconveniently located interventions. Latinos and other minorities are also less likely to possess the resources that would allow them to circumvent access issues"[2]. Therefore, my online meditation platform allows students, unemployed, and low-income Latinxs to apply for full scholarships and low-cost options.

Practices.

Research from Teasdale et al. and Dobkin et al.[1] explains that in mindfulness-based program (MBP) adaptations the creator needs to know the importance of explicit clarity regarding the core intentions of the MBP for the specific context and targeted participants. MBP developers should base the development in a clearly articulated aim and intention regarding the benefit and relevance of the program for a particular context and/or population.[1]

Because of this, I decided to be as clear and precise as possible. For example, I include a section called "Is this for me?" in the guidebook; this section specifically asks the reader to answer a couple of questions that can help determine if the book is good for them. Also, there is another one titled "Why *pertenæcer?*" In this section, I expand on the intention and relevance of the manual for Latinx immigrants in the United States.

Mindfulness can indeed be used as a tool for stress reduction, according to Kirmayer's[2] research on the meaning of mindfulness meditation in a cultural context and the usage of it in conventional psychiatry and psychology interventions. The author explains that in conventional treatment, although mindfulness is "presented as treatment for chronic stress-related medical and psychological conditions, the focus in MBSR is less on the symptom reduction than a transformation of the person's attitude towards the illness"[2]. Research from Chiesa and Serretti;

196

Hunot et al.; Keng, Smoski, and Robins; and Sedlmeier et al.[2] highlights that "Mindfulness-based therapeutic techniques have become popular methods for stress reduction and the treatment of chronic pain, anxiety, and depression. Systematic reviews, and meta-analyses of clinical trials provide evidence of the efficacy of mindfulness-based interventions for a wide range of conditions"[2]. Hence, the decision to use mindfulness-based practices and meditations as a method to help reduce acculturative stress; and as mentioned earlier in the paper, the main Buddhist derived teaching used in the guidebook is *Vipassana*, known as insight meditation.

García-Campayo, Demarzo, Shonin, and Van Gordon's[3] findings encourage the use of mindfulness of the body exercises. The authors observed that Latin patients relate better to a scan or mindful body movement practices, noting that "Latin individuals typically have fewer reservations in being tactile, showing their bodies, or in making direct eye-contact (i.e., without being uncomfortable). This characteristic is almost certainly linked to willingness to express feelings and the benefit of stronger social networks"[3]. The same authors also noticed positive engagement to meditation postures required for Mindfulness and Compassion training. Hence the emphasis in the guidebook to invite the participant to practice in relational and body-based mindfulness practices each week.

Randomized trials of MBSR from Jain et al., Kabat-Zinn et al., and Speca, Carlos, Goodey, and Angen[4] found that MBSR was effective in decreasing symptoms of stress, worry, and rumination[4]. Also, studies from Astin; Shapiro, Astin, Bishop, and Cordova; and Williams et al.[4] found that MBSR helped with self-reported distress[4]. Klatt, Buckworth, and Malarkey; and Shapiro, Schwartz, and Bonner[4] mention another benefit from MBSR, which was that people who had participated in MBSR training were more empathetic, and self-compassionate[4], hence the guidebook's dedicated focus on developing compassion and self-compassion, as well as inviting body-movement based mindfulness practices through the weeks. García-Campayo, Demarzo, Shonin, and Van Gordon[3] also recommend that Compassion practices should be emphasized in Latin populations[3]. Therefore, Buddhist derived Compassion and self-compassion concepts, and practices are emphasized throughout the book; more specifically, week six is dedicated to learning about compassion and self-compassion, along with guided meditations.

The guidebook includes mindfulness concepts such as interconnectedness, and it is presented as a new perspective that can help work with feelings of not belonging. Therefore, this interconnectedness is worked along with empathy and loving-kindness to work towards a mindset of belonging. As explained in Torres[5], the ability to mesh, relate, and create relationships with both cultures, the American and the native one, is a sign that this person can succeed in navigating both cultures[4]. Therefore, "this sense of interconnectedness becomes an important component of not only acquiring cultural content but establishing social support networks"[5]. Furthermore, the same article concludes that "[t]he ability to engage in a balanced set of intercultural competencies may be a mechanism that buffers Latinos from increased psychological problems"[5]. Week seven is completely dedicated to interconnectedness and empathy. Empathy is the best way to explain a sense of our connection with other people. Thus, the meditation section for this week is based on loving-kindness meditation; it "establishes a deep sense of positive interconnectedness to others, regardless of their group membership, that is incompatible with social biases and thus can potentially inhibit automatically activated biases"[6]. The overall goal is the journey of these late-immigrant Latinx under acculturative stress.

MBSR has also shown to be effective in increasing the ability to self-regulate as found in research from Tacon, McComb, Caldera, and Randolph[4]. In week four, Self-regulation is a concept that is introduced to the readers. The goal is to provide self-regulation as a tool to work through negative emotions emerging from discrimination or acculturative stressors. As it was revealed in research from Paradies; and Williams, Neighbors, and Jackson, discrimination has been associated with depression, psychological distress, and anxiety[4]. It is important to note that the prolonged effects of acculturative stressors lead to the development of mental illnesses that may be treatable with mindfulness practices. The expectation is to provide this training before these mental illnesses have caused brain imbalances, hence the main motivator to develop this mental hygiene guidebook.

Research also found that it was effective to "[e]mphasize interpersonal mindfulness: Given that family plays an important role in Latin society, interpersonal mindfulness (i.e., that necessitates awareness of one's own as well as others' emotions) tends to be well-received by Latin participants"[3]. Along with familyism, there is an encouragement to use personalization. Roth explains that the "primary barrier to enrolling in an MBSR program for minority populations is a lack of rapport with or mistrust of health care providers"[4]. These were primary considerations both from the mindfulness perspective and from the cultural values perspective; as explained earlier, the guidebook includes mindfulness exercises that welcome connection with family, friends, and loved ones - plus my personal story and the option to connect with me via the online go-along session.

Furthermore, research advocates keeping in mind religious concerns that participants may have while practicing meditation and mindfulness. As shared in García-Campayo, Demarzo, Shonin, and Van

Gordon[3] research instructors may become aware of the effect of religious influences; "[the] Catholic Church may not advocate certain yoga or mind-body practices due to their Buddhist and/or Hinduist influences"[3]. Therefore, week six focuses on teaching how mental hygiene, mindfulness, and meditation are not religious practices. Also, week three is dedicated to learning about mindfulness, its universality, and its primary use as a mental health hygiene method.

Kirmayer[2] advocates that mindfulness interventions, such as this guidebook, should consider that,

> An engaged ethical practice would work against these kinds of suffering: addressing through medicine the aspects of suffering that arise from the breakdowns of our brains and bodies; applying mindfulness and insight to eliminate the secondary or adventitious suffering that arises from attachment to self; and acting politically to redress the 'tertiary' suffering that arises from the human abuse of human beings as manifested in poverty, inequality, and structural violence.[2]

The hope is that the guidebook helps to reduce the suffering caused by inequality and structural violence derived from the process of immigration and acculturation.

Engagement.

Ortiz[1] suggests the usage of testimonials in MBSR adaptations for Latinxs. Research in Ortiz's[1] paper from Smeets et al. and Sue and Zane show "that doubt regarding the perceived acceptability, credibility, and effectiveness of treatment options during initial clinical visits may be responsible for increased early attrition rates in treatment"[1]. The guidebook includes simplified details of benefits of mindfulness and meditation. So in case there is any doubt from the reader, all research and concepts have citations available in the notes section at the end of the guidebook. The reader is also encouraged and invited to try and test for themselves the effectiveness of practices.

Kambolis[2] studied "the factors that may contribute to the successful implementation of long-term meditation practice"[2]; in this research, three core themes were taken into consideration: The lived experience of the meditator, Personality factors, and adherence to a consistent meditation practice. The study came to find that, "while researchers are well on their way to identifying factors that may influence the success of a consistent meditation practice, there is little yet known about what works for whom and why."[2]. Therefore, this guidebook uses as reference various meditation and mindfulness practices that have been culturally-attuned according to research, what helped me, and what I think can help others in the process of building a sense of belonging and tools to cope with acculturative stress.

Effective Coping Strategies for Latinx

It was important also to research and identify what coping tools were active already within the Latinx community so I could also consider that. Cobb, Xie, and Sanders[1] examined coping strategies and their relationship with depression among undocumented Hispanic immigrants in the United States[1]. "The authors categorized coping strategies as problem-focused, active-emotional, or avoidant-emotional. Findings indicated that coping through 'prayer and meditation' (problem-focused), 'get comfort from someone' (active-emotional), and 'see bad things positively' (active-emotional) were more frequently used by undocumented Hispanics"[1]. These coping strategies are defined as,

Problem-focused coping involves changing or addressing the problem directly. Such coping is typically understood as an adaptive strategy that may include identifying and pursuing a plan of action or taking specific steps to deal with a problem. Emotion-focused coping involves managing one's emotions related to the problem, which can be active -emotional, whereby one confronts the problem directly, or avoidant-emotional, whereby one evades the issue.[1]

The first successful coping tool used by Latinxs in this research included the practice of prayer and meditation. In the guidebook, meditation practice is formally introduced in week three; however guided meditation starts from week one. Doubts and conflicts with religion are addressed in briefly in week three; however, they are discussed in more detail in week six. The second coping tool was the act of getting comfort from someone; the guidebook mimics this coping tool by inviting the reader to practice relational mindfulness practices. The third one was a change in perspective to see bad things positively; this tool has a whole week dedicated to it. Week three introduces mindfulness and meditation as new tools to change the perspective on thoughts and emotions.

The authors added that "Latinos also engage in avoidant coping, such as denial or doing things to take one's mind off the severity of a situation, which has been associated with higher levels of depression and anxiety among this group"[1]. The guidebook takes this into close consideration and hopes that the cultural adaptations and encouragement to join an online group can keep readers engaged and ready to complete the training.

Conclusion

This amazing venture into acculturative stress of Latinx immigrants like myself, made it evident that underneath the surface, all people want to belong. Especially those who migrate and leave behind family, friends, culture, traditions, language, etc. Belonging is a yearning present in every human being, and I believe we yearn to belong within ourselves, our families, our communities, and, most importantly, within our world. Acculturative stress primarily manifests with feelings of isolation and not belonging; these feelings arise due to the pressures of learning a new language, balancing differing cultural values, and having to negotiate between American and Latinx ways of daily living. On top of that Latinxs carry within deeply embedded stigmas around mental health, that keep them from reaching out or practicing mental health hygiene; and eventually this leads us to develop psychological distress.

My personal experience with battling psychological distress, stigmas, and feelings of not belonging, led me to share with others the tools that helped me and continue to help me cope with the process of being an immigrant. Even though most of the research visited in this paper lacks information on the variety of Latinx American cultures, it is important to say that all the visited cultural values, stigmas, and cultural competencies may or may not be true for everyone within this diverse group. However, as the author, daughter of immigrant parents, a past immigrant of the US, past Immigrant of Mexico, and current immigrant of Spain, I can say that these principles are an excellent representation of the essence behind the diverse Latinx cultures in the US.

Throughout the eight weeks of the guidebook, students learn about mindfulness and meditation as methods of mental hygiene. These methods are presented as tools to work with symptoms of acculturative stress. The teachings provide a new culturally-attuned approach and perspective for understanding and practicing the different mindfulness and meditation exercises. Participants specifically learn about mental health stigmas, the mind, self-regulation, emotions, cultivation of self-love, compassion, self-compassion, and overall how to nurture and cultivate feelings and mindsets of belonging to themselves, their families, their communities, their country, and the world.

Moreover, participants in the program mainly follow the Paulo Freire's pedagogical approach where "Knowledge emerges only through invention and reinvention, through the restless, impatient, continuing, hopeful inquiry human beings pursue in the world, with the world, and with each other"[1]. In other words, students answer reflection questions each week to help the process of identifying negative habits and behaviors, so they can start replacing them with new culturally-attuned perspectives, habits, and behaviors.

The guidebook is not intended to be a method for achieving ultimate happiness. Instead, my primary goal as the author and as a mindfulness instructor and practitioner is to help end some of the pain and suffering present in less-acculturated-late-immigrant Latinx in the US. Lastly, I hope that my work can help reduce stigma and increase acceptance and engagement in mental health care and hygiene from the Latinx immigrant community in the United States.

Notes

Dichos (Sayings)

a. Retrieved from:

https://www.inmigracion.com/blog/hh-dichos-refranes-latinoamericanos/

https://www.youtube.com/watch?v=ZQVGByvl_FA

https://www.aboutespanol.com/dichos-y-refranes-latinoamericanos-1771587

https://quemas.mamaslatinas.com/inspiration/106466/mes_de_la_herencia_hispana

About this Guidebook

Is this for Me?

1. Guerra, G., & Orbea, G. (2015). The argument against the use of the term 'Latinx'. UWIRE Text.

Retrieved from http://ezproxyles.flo.org/login?url=https://search-ebscohost-com.ezproxyles.flo.org/login.aspx?direct=true&db=edsggo&AN=edsgcl.434993429&site=eds-live&scope=site

2. Steinmetz, K. (2018). Why 'Latinx' is succeeding while other gender-neutral terms fail to catch on. Time, (14).

Retrieved from http://ezproxyles.flo.org/login?url=https://search-ebscohostcom.ezproxyles.flo.org/
login.aspx?direct=true&db=edsgea&AN=edsgcl.53341
7615&site=eds-live&scope=site

3. Silva, M. A., Paris, M., & Añez, L. M. (2017). Camino: Integrating context in the mental health assessment of

immigrant Latinos. Professional Psychology: Research and Practice, 48(6), Page 456.

Why Pertenæcer?
1. Retrieved from https://en.wikipedia.org/wiki/%C3%86

How to Use this Guidebook
1. Magee, R. (June 1, 2015). The Way of ColorInsight: Understanding Race and Law Effectively Through Mindfulness-
Based ColorInsight Practices. Georgetown Law Journal of Modern Critical Race Perspectives, January 2016; Univ.
of San Francisco Law Research Paper No. 2015-19. Page 50.

Learning and Teaching Approach
1. Freire, P. (1996). Pedagogy of the oppressed (revised). New York: Continuum. Page 72.

2. Retrieved from http://www.juanabordas.com/your-grand-mother-was-right/

Week 1 - How Are You?
1. Retrieved from https://www.anxietycentre.com/anxiety-attack-symptoms.shtml

What is Mental Health and the Mind?
1. Lama, D. Pacificar la mente: Meditación sobre las cuatro nobles verdades del buda [Pacifying the mind:
Meditation on the four noble truths of the Buddha]. Barcelona, Spain: Ediciones Paidos Iberica, S.A. Page 15.

2. Retrieved from https://www.webmd.com/anxiety-panic/guide/anxiety-disorders#1

3. Torres, L., Driscoll, M. W., & Voell, M. (2012). Discrimination, acculturation, acculturative Stress, and Latino
    psychological distress: A moderated mediational model. Cultural Diversity & Ethnic Minority Psychology, 18(1),
    17-25.'

4. Siegel, D. J. (2013). Mindfulness, Mindsight and the Brain: What is Mind and Mental Health? [Video]. Phoenix, AZ:
    Milton H. Erickson Foundation.

5. Retrieved from https://www.psychologytoday.com/us/blog/struck-living/201202/mental-hygiene-preventative-
    care-mental-illness

Mental Health in the Latinx Immigrant Community

1. Turner, E. A., & Llamas, J. D. (n.d). The role of therapy fears, ethnic identity, and spirituality on access to mental
    health treatment among Latino college students. Psychological Services, 14(4), 524-530.

2. Torres, L. (2009). Latino definitions of success: A cultural model of intercultural competence. Hispanic Journal of
    Behavioral Sciences, 31(4), 576-593. Page 576-577.

What is Stress?

1. Retrieved from http://www.stress.org.uk/what-is-stress/

2. Asurero, A. M. (2008). Con rumbo propio: Disfruta de la vida sin estrés [Your own course: Enjoy life without
stress] (20th ed.). Barcelona, Spain: Plataforma Editorial. Page 47-48.

What is Acculturative Stress?

1. Craft, S., Crone, T., DeLeon, M., & Ajayi, A. (2018). Perceived and personal mental health stigma in Latino and
African American college students. Frontiers in Public Health, 6(49), 1-10.

2. Torres, L., Driscoll, M. W., & Voell, M. (2012). Discrimination, acculturation, acculturative Stress, and Latino
psychological distress: A moderated mediational model. Cultural Diversity & Ethnic Minority Psychology, 18(1), '
17-25.'

Week 2 – Connecting with My Story, My Ancestors, and My Culture

1. Torres, L. (2009). Latino definitions of success: A cultural model of intercultural competence. Hispanic Journal of
Behavioral Sciences, 31(4), 576-593.
Torres, L., Driscoll, M. W., & Voell, M. (2012). Discrimination, acculturation, acculturative Stress, and Latino
psychological distress: A moderated mediational model. Cultural Diversity & Ethnic Minority Psychology, 18(1),
17-25.

Immigration Circumstances

1. Bordas, J. (2012). Salsa, soul, and spirit: Leadership for a multicultural age (2nd ed.). San Francisco, CA: Berrett-
Koehler Publishers. Page 2.

Balancing and Negotiating Cultural Values

1. Oyserman, D., & Lee, S. S. (2008). Does culture influence what and how we think? Effects of priming individualism
   and collectivism. Psychological Bulletin, 134(2), Pages 312-313.
   Bordas, J. (2012). Salsa, soul, and spirit: Leadership for a multicultural age (2nd ed.). San Francisco, CA: Berrett-
   Koehler Publishers. Page 46-53.

2. Carteret, M. (2011, March 15). Cultural values of Latino patients and families. Retrieved from
   http://www.dimensionsofculture.com/2011/03/cultural-values-of-latino-patients-and-families/

3. Bordas, J. (2012). Salsa, soul, and spirit: Leadership for a multicultural age (2nd ed.). San Francisco, CA: Berrett-
   Koehler Publishers. Page 55-56.

4. Bordas, J. (2012). Salsa, soul, and spirit: Leadership for a multicultural age (2nd ed.). San Francisco, CA: Berrett-
   Koehler Publishers. Page 46-53.

Learning a New Language

1. Bordas, J. (2012). Salsa, soul, and spirit: Leadership for a multicultural age (2nd ed.). San Francisco, CA: Berrett-
   Koehler Publishers. Page 41-42.

2. https://www.uscis.gov/us-citizenship/naturalization-test/naturalization-oath-allegiance-united-states-america

Battling Feelings of Isolation and Not Belonging

1. Brown, B. (2017). Braving the wilderness: The quest for true belonging and the courage to stand alone. London,
   UK: Penguin Random House. Page 32.
2. Fuertes, J. N., & Westbrook, F. D. (1996). Using the social, attitudinal, familial, and environmental (S.A.F.E.)
   acculturation stress scale to asses the adjustment needs of Hispanic college students. American Counseling
   Association, 29(2), 67.

3. Brown, B. (2017). Braving the wilderness: The quest for true belonging and the courage to stand alone. London,
   UK: Penguin Random House. Page 52.

MINDFULNESS ACTIVITY:
1. Bordas, J. (2012). Salsa, soul, and spirit: Leadership for a multicultural age (2nd ed.). San Francisco, CA: Berrett-
   Koehler Publishers. Page 42 -43.

Week 3 – Embracing a New Perspective
1. Modestini, E. (March 14, 2016). Vinyasa 101: 5 things you didn't know about vinyasa yoga. Retrieved from
   https://www.yogajournal.com/yoga-101/vinyasa-101-5-things-you-didnt-know-about-vinyasa-yoga   ·

What is Mindfulness?
1. Kabat-Zinn, J. (2005). Coming to our senses. Healing ourselves and the world through mindfulness. New York,
   NY: Hyperion. Page 108.

2. Kirmayer, L., (2015). Mindfulness in cultural context. Transcultural Psychiatry, 52(4), Page 447.

What is a Mindfulness Practice?
1. Kirmayer, L., (2015). Mindfulness in cultural context. Transcultural Psychiatry, 52(4), Page 453.

2. Tan, C., (2012). Search inside yourself: The unexpected path to achieving success, happiness (and world peace).
   New York, NY: HarperOne. Page 52-53.

What is Meditation?
1. Kirmayer, L., (2015). Mindfulness in cultural context. Transcultural Psychiatry, 52(4), Page 448.

2. Salzberg, S. (2010). El secreto de la felicidad auténtica. El poder de la meditación, Aprende a ser feliz en 28
   días. [Real Happiness: The Power of Meditation; A 28-Day Program]. Barcelona, Spain: Zenith. Page 27-29.

3. Salzberg, S. (2010). El secreto de la felicidad auténtica. El poder de la meditación, Aprende a ser feliz en 28
   días. [Real Happiness: The Power of Meditation; A 28-Day Program]. Barcelona, Spain: Zenith. Page 21.

Benefits of Mindfulness and Meditation
1. Salzberg, S. (2010). El secreto de la felicidad auténtica. El poder de la meditación, Aprende a ser feliz en 28
   días. [Real Happiness: The Power of Meditation; A 28-Day Program]. Barcelona, Spain: Zenith. Page 34-40.
   Santorelli, S. F., Kabat-Zinn, J., Blacker, M., Meleo-Meyer, F. and Koerbel, L. (2017). Mindfulness-based stress

reduction (MBSR) authorized curriculum guide. Retrieved from http://www.umassmed.edu/cfm/training/mbsr-curriculum. Page 7, 11, 49.

Davis, D. M., & Hayes, J. A. (2011). What are the benefits of mindfulness? A practice review of psychotherapy-related research. Psychotherapy, 48(2), Page 198.

Mindfulness and Meditation as Mental Hygiene Tools

1. Miville, M. L., Arredondo, P., Consoli, A. J., Santiago-Rivera, A., Delgado-Romero, E. A., Fuentes, M. A., & ... Cervantes, J. M. (2017). Liderazgo: Culturally grounded leadership and the National Latina/o Psychological Association. The Counseling Psychologist, 45(6), p. 840.

2. Carteret, M. (2011, March 15). Cultural values of Latino patients and families. Retrieved from http://www.dimensionsofculture.com/2011/03/cultural-values-of-latino-patients-and-families/. p. 3

3. Bermúdez, J. M., Kirkpatrick, D., Hecker, L., & Torres-Robles, C. (2010). Describing Latinos families and their help-seeking attitudes: Challenging the family therapy literature. Contemporary Family Therapy: An International Journal, 32(2). Page 158-159.

Mindfulness of Body

1. Asurero, A. M. (2008). Con rumbo propio: Disfruta de la vida sin estrés [Your own course: Enjoy life without stress] (20th ed.). Barcelona, Spain: Plataforma Editorial. Page 65.

Week 4 – Reigning the Mind and Body
What are Mental Health Stigmas?

1. Craft, S., Crone, T., DeLeon, M., & Ajayi, A. (2018). Perceived and personal mental health stigma in Latino and
   African American college students. Frontiers in Public Health, 6(49), Page 1.

2. Fripp, J. A., & Carlson, R. G. (2017). Exploring the influence of attitude and stigma on participation of African
   American and Latino populations in mental health services. Journal of Multicultural Counseling and
   Development, 45(2), Page 83.

3. Guarnaccia, P. J., Martinez, I., & Acosta, H. (2005). Mental health in the Hispanic immigrant community. Journal of
   Immigrant & Refugee Services, 3(1/2), Page 35.

4. Turner, E. A., & Llamas, J. D. (n.d). The role of therapy fears, ethnic identity, and spirituality on access to mental
   health treatment among Latino college students. Psychological Services, 14(4), Page 525, 527, 528.
   Guarnaccia, P. J., Martinez, I., & Acosta, H. (2005). Mental health in the Hispanic immigrant community. Journal of
   Immigrant & Refugee Services, 3(1/2), Page 24, 26, 27, 34, 35, 36.
   Fripp, J. A., & Carlson, R. G. (2017). Exploring the influence of attitude and stigma on participation of African
   American and Latino populations in mental health services. Journal of Multicultural Counseling and
   Development, 45(2), Page 83.
   García-Campayo, J., Demarzo, M., Shonin, E., & Van Gordon, W. (2017). How do cultural factors influence the

teaching and practice of mindfulness and compassion in Latin countries? Frontiers in Psychology, 8, Page 2.

Bravo, A. (2018). Do the expressive arts therapies aid in identity formation and authenticity in the Latina

community? A community engagement project (Unpublished doctoral dissertation). Retrieved from

DigitalCommons@Lesley. Page 9.

5. Craft, S., Crone, T., DeLeon, M., & Ajayi, A. (2018). Perceived and personal mental health stigma in Latino and

African American college students. Frontiers in Public Health, 6(49), Page 2, 3.

Fripp, J. A., & Carlson, R. G. (2017). Exploring the influence of attitude and stigma on participation of African

American and Latino populations in mental health services. Journal of Multicultural Counseling and Development,

45(2), Page 83.

García-Campayo, J., Demarzo, M., Shonin, E., & Van Gordon, W. (2017). How do cultural factors influence the teaching and practice of mindfulness and compassion in Latin countries? Frontiers in Psychology, 8, Page 2.

Guarnaccia, P. J., Martinez, I., & Acosta, H. (2005). Mental health in the Hispanic immigrant community. Journal of   Immigrant & Refugee Services, 3(1/2), Page 34, 36, 37, 40.

6. Guarnaccia, P. J., Martinez, I., & Acosta, H. (2005). Mental health in the Hispanic immigrant community. Journal of

Immigrant & Refugee Services, 3(1/2), Page 36.

Identify Mental Habits and Patterns
1. Tolle, E. (2005). A new earth: Awakening to your life's purpose. New York, NY: Penguin Group. Page 30.

2. Asurero, A. M. (2008). Con rumbo propio: Disfruta de la vida sin estrés [Your own course: Enjoy life without
stress] (20th ed.). Barcelona, Spain: Plataforma Editorial. Page 74.

3. Tolle, E. (2005). A new earth: Awakening to your life's purpose. New York, NY: Penguin Group. Page 32.

What are Stressors?
1. Tan, C., (2012). Search inside yourself: The unexpected path to achieving success, happiness (and world peace).
New York, NY: HarperOne. Page 116.

Self-regulation
1. Tan, C., (2012). Search inside yourself: The unexpected path to achieving success, happiness (and world peace).
New York, NY: HarperOne. Page 104-105.

2. Asurero, A. M. (2008). Con rumbo propio: Disfruta de la vida sin estrés [Your own course: Enjoy life without
stress] (20th ed.). Barcelona, Spain: Plataforma Editorial P. 103-108
Tan, C., (2012). Search inside yourself: The unexpected path to achieving success, happiness (and world peace).
New York, NY: HarperOne. Page 103-106.

MINDFULNESS PRACTICE #2
1. Tan, C., (2012). Search inside yourself: The unexpected path to achieving success, happiness (and world peace).

New York, NY: HarperOne. Page 116-117.

Week 5 – Getting to Know Emotions
1. Biblia de las Américas (Americas Bible). Proverb 17:22. Retrieved from: https://bibliaparalela.com/proverbs/17-
22.htm

2. Cherry, K. (December 17, 2018). The 3 key elements that make up emotion. *Verywell Mind.* Retrieved from
https://www.verywellmind.com/what-are-emotions-2795178

3. Asurero, A. M. (2008). Con rumbo propio: Disfruta de la vida sin estrés [Your own course: Enjoy life without
stress] (20th ed.). Barcelona, Spain: Plataforma Editorial. Page 94.

What is an Emotion?
1. Goleman, D. (1995). Emotional Intelligence: Why it can matter more than IQ. New york, NY: Bantam Books. Page
6.

2. Tan, C., (2012). Search inside yourself: The unexpected path to achieving success, happiness (and world peace).
New York, NY: HarperOne. Page 127.

3. Goleman, D. (1995). Emotional Intelligence: Why it can matter more than IQ. New york, NY: Bantam Books. Page
39.

4. Asurero, A. M. (2008). Con rumbo propio: Disfruta de la vida sin estrés [Your own course: Enjoy life without
stress] (20th ed.). Barcelona, Spain: Plataforma Editorial. Page 95.

5. Asurero, A. M. (2008). Con rumbo propio: Disfruta de la vida sin estrés [Your own course: Enjoy life without
   stress] (20th ed.). Barcelona, Spain: Plataforma Editorial. Page 100.

Understanding Fear

1. Asurero, A. M. (2008). Con rumbo propio: Disfruta de la vida sin estrés [Your own course: Enjoy life without
   stress] (20th ed.). Barcelona, Spain: Plataforma Editorial. Page 95.

2. Asurero, A. M. (2008). Con rumbo propio: Disfruta de la vida sin estrés [Your own course: Enjoy life without
   stress] (20th ed.). Barcelona, Spain: Plataforma Editorial. Page 96.
   Goleman, D. (1995). Emotional Intelligence: Why it can matter more than IQ. New york, NY: Bantam Books. Page
   331.

3. Retrieved from https://www.umassmed.edu/cfm/mindfulness-based-programs/mbsr-courses/about-mbsr/
   Retrieved from https://www.verywellmind.com/benefits-of-mindfulness-based-stress-reduction-88861
   Retrieved from https://www.mindfulnessstudies.com/mindfulness/evidence/

4. Brown, B. (2017). Braving the wilderness: The quest for true belonging and the courage to stand alone. London,
   UK: Penguin Random House. Page 56.

5. Brown, B. (2017). Braving the wilderness: The quest for true belonging and the courage to stand alone. London,
   UK: Penguin Random House. Page 69.

6. Brown, B. (2017). Braving the wilderness: The quest for true belonging and the courage to stand alone. London,
   UK: Penguin Random House. Page 66-67.

Understanding Anger

1. Asurero, A. M. (2008). Con rumbo propio: Disfruta de la vida sin estrés [Your own course: Enjoy life without
   stress] (20th ed.). Barcelona, Spain: Plataforma Editorial. Page 97-98.

2. Goleman, D. (1995). Emotional Intelligence: Why it can matter more than IQ. New york, NY: Bantam Books. Page
   331.

3. Brown, B. (2017). Braving the wilderness: The quest for true belonging and the courage to stand alone. London,
   UK: Penguin Random House. Page 67-69.

Understanding Sadness

1. Asurero, A. M. (2008). Con rumbo propio: Disfruta de la vida sin estrés [Your own course: Enjoy life without
   stress] (20th ed.). Barcelona, Spain: Plataforma Editorial. Page 98.

2. Goleman, D. (1995). Emotional Intelligence: Why it can matter more than IQ. New york, NY: Bantam Books. Page
   331.

Understanding Joy

1. Asurero, A. M. (2008). Con rumbo propio: Disfruta de la vida sin estrés [Your own course: Enjoy life without
   stress] (20th ed.). Barcelona, Spain: Plataforma Editorial. Page 100-101.

Mindfulness of Emotions
1. Kabat-Zinn, J. (2005). Coming to our senses. Healing ourselves and the world through mindfulness. New York,
   NY: Hyperion. Page 108.

2. Asurero, A. M. (2008). Con rumbo propio: Disfruta de la vida sin estrés [Your own course: Enjoy life without
   stress] (20th ed.). Barcelona, Spain: Plataforma Editorial. Page 95-101.

3. Goleman, D. (1995). Emotional Intelligence: Why it can matter more than IQ. New york, NY: Bantam Books. Page
   7-8.

Week 6 – Belonging in Me, My Family, and My Community
1. Hays, P. (n.d.). An International Perspective on the Adaptation of CBT Across Cultures. Australian
   Psychologist, 49(1), 17–18.

What is Compassion?
1. Rothberg, D. (2006). The engaged spiritual life: A buddhist approach to transforming ourselves and the
   world. UK: Windhorse Publications. Page 83.

2. Feldman, C. (2017). Boundless Heart: The buddha's path of kindness, compassion, joy, and equanimity. Boulder,
   CO: Shambala Publications. Page 131.

Compassion in Spirituality and Religion
1. Jalon, G. (n.d.) Entrevista con Davidji [Interview with Davidji]. Retrieved from: https://cosas.com.ec/davidji

-%C2%93si-rezar-es-hablar-con-dios-meditar-es-escucharlo%C2%94/

2. Campesino, M., & Schwartz, G. E. (2006). Spirituality among Latinas/os: implications of culture in
   conceptualization and measurement. ANS. Advances in nursing science, 29(1), Page 70.

3. Kirmayer, L., (2015). Mindfulness in cultural context. Transcultural Psychiatry, 52(4), Page 449.

4. Bravo, A. (2018). Do the expressive arts therapies aid in identity formation and authenticity in the Latina
   community? A community engagement project (Unpublished doctoral dissertation). Retrieved from
   DigitalCommons@Lesley. Page 9.

Cultivating Compassion
1. Bordas, J. (2012). Salsa, soul, and spirit: Leadership for a multicultural age (2nd ed.). San Francisco, CA: Berrett-
   Koehler Publishers. Page 67.

2. Kirmayer, L., (2015). Mindfulness in cultural context. Transcultural Psychiatry, 52(4), Page 453.

3. Kabat-Zinn, J. (2005). Coming to our senses. Healing ourselves and the world through mindfulness. New York,
   NY: Hyperion. Page 350 - 351.

4. Magee, R. (June 1, 2015). The Way of ColorInsight: Understanding Race and Law Effectively Through Mindfulness-

Based ColorInsight Practices. Georgetown Law Journal of Modern Critical Race Perspectives, January 2016; Univ.
of San Francisco Law Research Paper No. 2015-19. Page 21.

5. Neff, K. (n.d.). Why women need fierce self-compassion. Retrieved from https://self-compassion.org/women-
fierce-self-compassion/

6. García-Campayo, J., Demarzo, M., Shonin, E., & Van Gordon, W. (2017). How do cultural factors influence the
teaching and practice of mindfulness and compassion in Latin countries? Frontiers in Psychology, 8, Page 3.

MEDITATION PRACTICE
1. Kang, Y., Gray, J. R., & Dovidio, J. F. (2014). The nondiscriminating heart: lovingkindness meditation training
decreases implicit intergroup bias. Journal of Experimental Psychology General, 143(3), Page 1307.

Week 7 – We are One World
1. Torres, L. (2009). Latino definitions of success: A cultural model of intercultural competence. Hispanic Journal of
Behavioral Sciences, 31(4), 576-593. Page 589.

2. Bermúdez, J. M., Kirkpatrick, D., Hecker, L., & Torres-Robles, C. (2010). Describing Latinos families and their
help-seeking attitudes: Challenging the family therapy literature. *Contemporary Family Therapy: An International Journal, 32*(2), 155-172.

What is Interconnectedness?

1. Petty, E (Ed.). (July 2017). Social Justice, Inner Work & Contemplative Practice: Lessons & Directions for Multiple Fields. ICEA Journal, 1(1), Page 121. Retrieved from http://www.contemplativemind.org/files/ICEA_vol1_2017.pdf.

2. Torres, L. (2009). Latino definitions of success: A cultural model of intercultural competence. Hispanic Journal of Behavioral Sciences, 31(4), 576-593. Page 586.

Understanding Empathy

1. Tan, C., (2012). Search inside yourself: The unexpected path to achieving success, happiness (and world peace). New York, NY: HarperOne. Page 160.

2. Goleman, D. (1995). Emotional Intelligence: Why it can matter more than IQ. New york, NY: Bantam Books. Page 109.

Cultivating Empathy

1. Goleman, D. (1995). Emotional Intelligence: Why it can matter more than IQ. New york, NY: Bantam Books. Page 110.

Transforming Shame

1. Brown, B. (January 14, 213). Shame v. Guilt. Retrieved from https://brenebrown.com/blog/2013/01/14/shame-v-guilt/

2. Brown, B. (2012) Listeninig to shame. TED talks. Retrieved from

https://www.ted.com/talks/brene_brown_listening_to_shame/transcript?language=en#t-272402

MEDITATION PRACTICE:
1. Magee, R. (June 1, 2015). The Way of ColorInsight: Understanding Race and Law Effectively Through Mindfulness-
   Based ColorInsight Practices. Georgetown Law Journal of Modern Critical Race Perspectives, January 2016; Univ.
   of San Francisco Law Research Paper No. 2015-19. Page 48.

Week 8 – Belonging in Life Mindfully
1. Retrieved from https://www.youtube.com/watch?v=ZQVGByvl_FA

What is Hope?
1. Goleman, D. (1995). Emotional Intelligence: Why it can matter more than IQ. New york, NY: Bantam Books. Page
   97-98.

What is Optimism?
1. Goleman, D. (1995). Emotional Intelligence: Why it can matter more than IQ. New york, NY: Bantam Books. Page
   99.
2. Goleman, D. (1995). Emotional Intelligence: Why it can matter more than IQ. New york, NY: Bantam Books. Page
   100.

Appendix A – Stress-related Idioms in Latinx Community
1. Retrieved from

https://www.ihs.gov/telebehavioral/includes/themes/newihstheme/display_objects/documents/slides/
   nationalchildandadolescent/2013/hispanicmentalhealth0213.pdf

2. Guarnaccia, P. J., Martinez, I., & Acosta, H. (2005). Mental health in the Hispanic immigrant community. Journal of Immigrant & Refugee Services, 3(1/2), Page 36-38.

3. Silva, M. A., Paris, M., & Añez, L. M. (2017). Camino: Integrating context in the mental health assessment of immigrant Latinos. Professional Psychology: Research and Practice, 48(6), Page 457.

Appendix B - Research-based benefits from Mindfulness and

Mindfulness Based Stress Reduction Programs

1. Retrieved from https://www.umassmed.edu/cfm/mindfulness-based-programs/mbsr-courses/about-mbsr/

2. Retrieved from https://www.verywellmind.com/benefits-of-mindfulness-based-stress-reduction-88861

3. Retrieved from https://www.mindfulnessstudies.com/mindfulness/evidence/

Usage of Latinx through the Guidebook
1.Steinmetz, K. (2018). Why 'Latinx' is succeeding while other gender-neutral terms fail to
catch on. *Time*, (14). Retrieved from
http://ezproxyles.flo.org/login?url=https://search-ebscohostcom.ezproxyles.flo.org/login.aspx?direct=true&db=edsgea&AN=edsgcl.53341
7615&site=eds-live&scope=site

2. Carteret, M. (2011, March 15). Cultural values of Latino patients and families. Retrieved from http://www.dimensionsofculture.com/2011/03/cultural-values-of-latino-patients-and-families/

Defining the Audience within the Latinx Immigrant Community in the United States
1. Turner, E. A., & Llamas, J. D. (n.d). The role of therapy fears, ethnic identity, and spirituality on access to mental health treatment among Latino college students. *Psychological Services, 14*(4), 524-530.

2. Falicov, C. J. (2009). Commentary: On the wisdom and challenges of culturally attuned   treatments for Latinos. *Family Process, 48*(2), 292-309.

3. Olano, H. A., Kachan, D., Tannenbaum, S. L., Mehta, A., Annane, D., & Lee, D. J. (2015).
Engagement in mindfulness practices by U.S. adults: Sociodemographic barriers. *Journal of Alternative & Complementary Medicine, 21*(2), 100-102.

4. Guarnaccia, P. J., Martinez, I., & Acosta, H. (2005). Mental health in the Hispanic
immigrant community. *Journal of Immigrant & Refugee Services, 3*(1/2), 21-46.

5. Bermúdez, J. M., Kirkpatrick, D., Hecker, L., & Torres-Robles, C. (2010). Describing Latinos

families and their help-seeking attitudes: Challenging the family therapy literature. *Contemporary Family Therapy: An International Journal, 32*(2), 155-172.

6. Torres, L. (2009). Latino definitions of success: A cultural model of intercultural
competence. *Hispanic Journal of Behavioral Sciences, 31*(4), 576-593.

7. Garcia, D.S. (2015). Acculturation: A core concept of Hispanic health research. *Hispanic   Health Care International, 13*(3), 115-118.

8. Silva, M. A., Paris, M., & Añez, L. M. (2017). Camino: Integrating context in the mental health assessment of immigrant Latinos. Professional *Psychology: Research and Practice, 48*(6), 453–460.

Acculturated Latinxs
1. Garcia, D.S. (2015). Acculturation: A core concept of Hispanic health research. *Hispanic   Health Care International, 13*(3), 115-118.

2. Craft, S., Crone, T., DeLeon, M., & Ajayi, A. (2018). Perceived and personal mental
health stigma in Latino and African American college students. *Frontiers in Public Health, 6*(49), 1-10.

3. Torres, L. (2009). Latino definitions of success: A cultural model of intercultural
competence. *Hispanic Journal of Behavioral Sciences, 31*(4), 576-593.

Less Acculturated Latinxs

1. Fuertes, J. N., & Westbrook, F. D. (1996). Using the social, attitudinal, familial, and environmental (S.A.F.E.) acculturation stress scale to assess the adjustment needs of
Hispanic college students. *American Counseling Association*, *29*(2), 67-76.

2. Craft, S., Crone, T., DeLeon, M., & Ajayi, A. (2018). Perceived and personal mental
health stigma in Latino and African American college students. *Frontiers in Public Health*, *6*(49), 1-10.

3. Guarnaccia, P. J., Martinez, I., & Acosta, H. (2005). Mental health in the Hispanic
immigrant community. *Journal of Immigrant & Refugee Services*, *3*(1/2), 21-46.

4. Torres, L., Driscoll, M. W., & Voell, M. (2012). Discrimination, acculturation, acculturative
Stress, and Latino psychological distress: A moderated meditational model. Cultural *Diversity & Ethnic Minority Psychology*, *18*(1), 17-25.

Socioeconomic Status and Social Mobility of Immigrant Latinxs

1.Rios-Salas, V., & Larson, A. (2015). Perceived discrimination, socioeconomic status, and mental health among Latino adolescents in US immigrant families. *Children and Youth Services Review*, *56*, 116-125.

2. Social mobility (n.d). In *Encyclopedia Britannica online*. Retrieved from
https://www.britannica.com/topic/social-mobility

3. Mendoza, S., Armbrister, A. N., & Abraido-Lanza, A. F. (n.d). Are you better off? Perceptions
of social mobility and satisfaction with care among Latina immigrants in the US. *Social Science & Medicine, 219*, 54–60.

Mindfulness and Meditation Versus Conventional Interventions for Coping with Acculturative Stress
1. Torres, L., Driscoll, M. W., & Voell, M. (2012). Discrimination, acculturation, acculturative
Stress, and Latino psychological distress: A moderated meditational model. Cultural *Diversity & Ethnic Minority Psychology, 18*(1), 17-25.

2. Torres, L. (2009). Latino definitions of success: A cultural model of intercultural
competence. *Hispanic Journal of Behavioral Sciences, 31*(4), 576-593.

3. About MBSR. (n.d) In Center for Mindfulness website. Retrieved from
https://www.umassmed.edu/cfm/mindfulness-based-programs/mbsr-courses/about-mbsr/

4. Silva, M. A., Paris, M., & Añez, L. M. (2017). Camino: Integrating context in the mental health assessment of immigrant
Latinos. Professional *Psychology: Research and Practice, 48*(6), 453–460.

Mindfulness and Meditation
1. Kabat-Zinn, J. (2005). *Coming to our senses. Healing ourselves and the world through mindfulness.* New York, NY: Hyperion.

2. Kirmayer, L., (2015). Mindfulness in cultural context. *Transcultural Psychiatry, 52*(4), 447-469.

3. Salzberg, S. (2010). *El secreto de la felicidad auténtica. El poder de la meditación, Aprende a ser feliz en 28 días.* [Real Happiness: The Power of Meditation; A 28-Day Program]. Barcelona, Spain: Zenith.

4. Tan, C., (2012). Search inside yourself: The unexpected path to achieving success, happiness (and world peace). New York, NY: HarperOne.

Mindfulness practices.
1. Kirmayer, L., (2015). Mindfulness in cultural context. *Transcultural Psychiatry, 52*(4), 447-469.

2. Tan, C., (2012). Search inside yourself: The unexpected path to achieving success, happiness (and world peace). New York, NY: HarperOne.

Healing Acculturative Stress of Late-immigrant Latinxs in the United States
1. Siegel, D. J. (2013). Mindfulness, Mindsight and the Brain: What is Mind and Mental Health?
[Video]. Phoenix, AZ: Milton H. Erickson Foundation.

2. Kirmayer, L., (2015). Mindfulness in cultural context. *Transcultural Psychiatry, 52*(4), 447-469.

Acknowledgment of Mental Health Stigmas

1. Fripp, J. A., & Carlson, R. G. (2017). Exploring the influence of attitude and stigma on
participation of African American and Latino populations in mental health services. *Journal of Multicultural Counseling and Development, 45*(2), 80-94.

2. Craft, S., Crone, T., DeLeon, M., & Ajayi, A. (2018). Perceived and personal mental
health stigma in Latino and African American college students. *Frontiers in Public Health, 6*(49), 1-10.

3. Guarnaccia, P. J., Martinez, I., & Acosta, H. (2005). Mental health in the Hispanic
immigrant community. *Journal of Immigrant & Refugee Services, 3*(1/2), 21-46.

Family-community generated mental health stigmas.

1. Oyserman, D., & Lee, S. S. (2008). Does culture influence what and how we think? Effects of
priming individualism and collectivism. *Psychological Bulletin, 134*(2), 311-342.

2. Carteret, M. (2011, March 15). Cultural values of Latino patients and families. Retrieved from
http://www.dimensionsofculture.com/2011/03/cultural-values-of-latino-patients-and-families/

3. Turner, E. A., & Llamas, J. D. (n.d). The role of therapy fears, ethnic identity, and spirituality on access to mental health treatment among Latino college students. *Psychological Services, 14*(4), 524-530.

4. García-Campayo, J., Demarzo, M., Shonin, E., & Van Gordon, W. (2017). How do cultural
factors influence the teaching and practice of mindfulness and compassion in Latin countries? *Frontiers in Psychology, 8*(1161), 1-4.

5. Bravo, A. (2018). *Do the expressive arts therapies aid in identity formation and authenticity
in the Latina community? A community engagement project* (Unpublished doctoral dissertation). Retrieved from DigitalCommons@Lesley.

6. Guarnaccia, P. J., Martinez, I., & Acosta, H. (2005). Mental health in the Hispanic
immigrant community. *Journal of Immigrant & Refugee Services, 3*(1/2), 21-46.

7. Fripp, J. A., & Carlson, R. G. (2017). Exploring the influence of attitude and stigma on
participation of African American and Latino populations in mental health services. *Journal of Multicultural Counseling and Development, 45*(2), 80-94.

Self-generated mental health stigmas.
1. Craft, S., Crone, T., DeLeon, M., & Ajayi, A. (2018). Perceived and personal mental
health stigma in Latino and African American college students. *Frontiers in Public Health, 6*(49), 1-10.

2. Fripp, J. A., & Carlson, R. G. (2017). Exploring the influence of attitude and stigma on

participation of African American and Latino populations in mental health services. *Journal of Multicultural Counseling and Development, 45*(2), 80-94.

3. García-Campayo, J., Demarzo, M., Shonin, E., & Van Gordon, W. (2017). How do cultural
factors influence the teaching and practice of mindfulness and compassion in Latin countries? *Frontiers in Psychology, 8*(1161), 1-4.

4. Guarnaccia, P. J., Martinez, I., & Acosta, H. (2005). Mental health in the Hispanic
immigrant community. *Journal of Immigrant & Refugee Services, 3*(1/2), 21-46.

Cultural Competence

1. Golonka Carmichael, N. (2012). Turning towards multicultural diversity competence in
dance/movement therapy. *American Journal of Dance Therapy, 34*(2), 99-113.

2. Guarnaccia, P. J., Martinez, I., & Acosta, H. (2005). Mental health in the Hispanic
immigrant community. *Journal of Immigrant & Refugee Services, 3*(1/2), 21-46.

3. Torres, L. (2009). Latino definitions of success: A cultural model of intercultural
competence. *Hispanic Journal of Behavioral Sciences, 31*(4), 576-593.

Cultural Values

1. Torres, L. (2009). Latino definitions of success: A cultural model of intercultural
competence. *Hispanic Journal of Behavioral Sciences, 31*(4), 576-593.

2. Miville, M. L., Arredondo, P., Consoli, A. J., Santiago-Rivera, A., Delgado-Romero, E. A.,
Fuentes, M. A., & ... Cervantes, J. M. (2017). Liderazgo: Culturally grounded leadership and the National Latina/o Psychological Association. *The Counseling Psychologist, 45*(6), 830-856.

3. Bermúdez, J. M., Kirkpatrick, D., Hecker, L., & Torres-Robles, C. (2010). Describing Latinos
families and their help-seeking attitudes: Challenging the family therapy literature. *Contemporary Family Therapy: An International Journal, 32*(2), 155-172.

4. Oyserman, D., & Lee, S. S. (2008). Does culture influence what and how we think? Effects of
priming individualism and collectivism. *Psychological Bulletin, 134*(2), 311-342.

5. Carteret, M. (2011, March 15). Cultural values of Latino patients and families. Retrieved from
http://www.dimensionsofculture.com/2011/03/cultural-values-of-latino-patients-and-families/
Mindfulness and Mindfulness-Based Stress Reduction in Latinx Communities

Length of practice.

1. García-Campayo, J., Demarzo, M., Shonin, E., & Van Gordon, W. (2017). How do cultural
factors influence the teaching and practice of mindfulness and compassion in Latin countries? *Frontiers in Psychology, 8*(1161), 1-4.

2. Crane, R. S., Brewer, J., Feldman, C., Kabat-Zinn, J., Santorelli, S., Williams, J. M. G., &
Kuyken, W. (2017). What defines mindfulness-based programs? the warp and the weft. *Psychological Medicine, 47*(6), 990-999.

Learning methods.

1. García-Campayo, J., Demarzo, M., Shonin, E., & Van Gordon, W. (2017). How do cultural
factors influence the teaching and practice of mindfulness and compassion in Latin countries? *Frontiers in Psychology, 8*(1161), 1-4.
2. Ortiz, J. A. (2015). *Bridging the gap: Adapting mindfulness-based stress reduction for Latino populations.* (Doctoral dissertation). Retrieved from ProQuest Dissertations and Theses database. (Order No. 3723541)

Practices.

1. Crane, R. S., Brewer, J., Feldman, C., Kabat-Zinn, J., Santorelli, S., Williams, J. M. G., &
Kuyken, W. (2017). What defines mindfulness-based programs? the warp and the weft. *Psychological Medicine, 47*(6), 990-999.

2. Kirmayer, L., (2015). Mindfulness in cultural context. *Transcultural Psychiatry, 52*(4), 447-469.

3. García-Campayo, J., Demarzo, M., Shonin, E., & Van Gordon, W. (2017). How do cultural

factors influence the teaching and practice of mindfulness and compassion in Latin countries? *Frontiers in Psychology, 8*(1161), 1-4.

4. Ortiz, J. A. (2015). *Bridging the gap: Adapting mindfulness-based stress reduction for Latino populations.* (Doctoral dissertation). Retrieved from ProQuest Dissertations and Theses database. (Order No. 3723541)

5. Torres, L. (2009). Latino definitions of success: A cultural model of intercultural
competence. *Hispanic Journal of Behavioral Sciences, 31*(4), 576-593.

6. Kang, Y., Gray, J. R., & Dovidio, J. F. (2014). The nondiscriminating heart: lovingkindness
meditation training decreases implicit intergroup bias. *Journal of Experimental*
Psychology General, 143(3), 1306–1313.

Engagement.
1. Ortiz, J. A. (2015). *Bridging the gap: Adapting mindfulness-based stress reduction for Latino populations.* (Doctoral dissertation). Retrieved from ProQuest Dissertations and Theses database. (Order No. 3723541)

2. Kambolis, D. (2017). Predictors of meditation success: A literature review. *HSOA Journal of*
Alternative, Complementary & Integrative Medicine, 3(3), 1-8.
Effective Coping Strategies for Latinx
1. Cobb, C. L., Xie, D., & Sanders, G. L. (2016). Coping styles and depression among
undocumented Hispanic immigrants. *Journal of Immigrant and Minority Health, 18*(4), 864-870.

Conclusion

1. Freire, P. (1996). *Pedagogy of the oppressed (revised)*. New York: Continuum.

Made in the USA
Middletown, DE
03 December 2020